Get Sorted!

www.skills4study.com – the leading study skills website

Palgrave Study Skills

Business Degree Success
Career Skills
Cite Them Right (9th edn)
Critical Thinking Skills (2nd edn)
e-Learning Skills (2nd edn)
The Exam Skills Handbook (2nd edn)
Great Ways to Learn Anatomy and
 Physiology (2nd edn)
How to Begin Studying English
 Literature (3rd edn)
How to Manage your Distance and
 Open Learning Course
How to Manage your Postgraduate
 Course
How to Study Foreign Languages
How to Study Linguistics (2nd edn)
How to Use Your Reading in Your Essays
 (2nd edn)
How to Write Better Essays (3rd edn)
How to Write Your Undergraduate
 Dissertation (2nd edn)
Improve Your Grammar
Information Skills
The International Student Handbook
IT Skills for Successful Study
The Mature Student's Guide to Writing
 (3rd edn)
The Mature Student's Handbook
The Palgrave Student Planner
Practical Criticism
Presentation Skills for Students (2nd
 edn)
The Principles of Writing in Psychology
Professional Writing (3rd edn)
Researching Online
Skills for Success (3rd edn)
The Student's Guide to Writing (3rd edn)
Study Skills Connected
The Study Skills Handbook (3rd edn)
Study Skills for International
 Postgraduates
Study Skills for Speakers of English as a
 Second Language
Studying History (3rd edn)

Studying Law (4th edn)
Studying Modern Drama (2nd edn)
Studying Psychology (2nd edn)
Teaching Study Skills and Supporting
 Learning
The Undergraduate Research Handbook
The Work-Based Learning Student
 Handbook (2nd edn)
Work Placements – a Survival Guide for
 Students
Write it Right (2nd edn)
Writing for Engineers (3rd edn)
Writing for Law
Writing for Nursing and Midwifery
 Students (2nd edn)
You2Uni

Pocket Study Skills

14 Days to Exam Success
Blogs, Wikis, Podcasts and More
Brilliant Writing Tips for Students
Completing Your PhD
Doing Research
Getting Critical (2nd edn)
Planning Your Essay (2nd edn)
Planning Your PhD
Posters and Presentations
Reading and Making Notes (2nd edn)
Referencing and Understanding
 Plagiarism
Reflective Writing
Report Writing
Science Study Skills
Studying with Dyslexia
Success in Groupwork
Time Management
Writing for University

Palgrave Research Skills

Authoring a PhD
The Foundations of Research (2nd edn)
The Good Supervisor (2nd edn)
The Postgraduate Research Handbook
 (2nd edn)

Get Sorted!

How to Make the Most of Your Student Experience

Jeff Gill and Will Medd

 macmillan education palgrave

First published 2015 by
PALGRAVE

Palgrave in the UK is an imprint of Macmillan Publishers Limited,
registered in England, company number 785998, of 4 Crinan Street,
London, N1 9XW.

Palgrave Macmillan in the US is a division of St Martin's Press LLC,
175 Fifth Avenue, New York, NY 10010.

Palgrave is a global imprint of the above companies and is represented
throughout the world.

Palgrave® and Macmillan® are registered trademarks in the United States,
the United Kingdom, Europe and other countries.

ISBN: 978-1-137-40593-7 paperback

This book is printed on paper suitable for recycling and made from fully
managed and sustained forest sources. Logging, pulping and manufacturing
processes are expected to conform to the environmental regulations of the
country of origin.

A catalogue record for this book is available from the British Library.

Printed in China

Contents

Acknowledgements

This book has come about through us both working together for quite some time. We are grateful to all those we have had the chance to work with as coaches, both on a one-to-one basis and in workshops. Much of what is in this book reflects what we've learnt by testing things out with people, as well as with ourselves, and finding out what makes a difference, and what seems to be less effective. The specific focus of this book – undergraduate university students – has been driven in part by funding from Lancaster University Alumni and Friends which enabled us to run 'Get Sorted' programmes at the university. We particularly thank Hilary Simmons and her team for their support in this. We also acknowledge the generosity of Open University Press/McGraw Hill in allowing us to adapt material from our previous book *Your PhD Coach*.

More specifically still has been the wonderful experience of working with students who have been willing to look differently at their situations and create a different experience for themselves. They have informed our thinking even if they don't know it! By working with them we have been able to put together ideas and examples that we hope now will help other students. Some of those students offered us examples of how they applied those ideas, and these are presented anonymously in the book, unedited. We are hugely grateful to those students and welcome their generosity in offering their experience for others to learn from. In particular we thank Adam, Craig, Georgia, Hannah, Harry, Luke, Rosie, Sophie, Pooky. Part of the challenge of writing a book like this is making it come to life – thanks so much to Daisy Emery and Helena Waudby for their patience, creativity and professionalism in bringing together the illustrations (and to Kate Dunbavan from Lancaster University, who orchestrated our funding for Daisy and Helena from UNITE With Business European Regional Development Fund). Thanks too for the excellent anonymous reviewers' feedback we received which helped us in developing the book, and to the team at Palgrave, in particular Suzannah Burywood and Bryony Ross for their editorial support and advice throughout, and Alec McAulay for meticulous proof reading. Finally, thanks to our friends and family for putting up with us through the process – we're sorry we sounded like your Gremlins at times!

Introduction – Get Sorted!

This book is about you. It's about how you can shape your university experience in the broadest sense based on what matters to you. 'I just need to get sorted' or 'I need to get my act together' seem to capture the sentiments of so many of the students we've worked with during workshops, coaching and lecturing. That's why we've written this book – to help you 'get sorted' and make the most from your experience.

Students describe their university experience in many ways. It's boring, exciting, confusing, having a laugh, satisfying, scary, fun, fine, heavy, pressurised, buzzing, disorganised, on top of things, disappointing, to name just a few. *Get Sorted* speaks to students with all kinds of experiences. It speaks to those who've lost the spark, and want to find a way to reignite the experience and get more from it. *Get Sorted* also speaks to those who are cruising, doing well, and yet want to push and find that bit more. And *Get Sorted* speaks to those who feel they're constantly up against a brick wall, feeling stuck and struggling to know how to move forwards.

For some, university life can feel disappointing, underwhelming, even boring. After all the promises of what university can offer, stories from your friends or parents of how they had the time of their lives, perhaps you're feeling disappointed! Perhaps you're wanting more from your subject, needing to boost your motivation, to meet new people, or engage with things that matter to you. If so, it seems a pity to just drift along and watch the time go by – what if you were to make it a time to remember?

For others, university life can be a struggle, overwhelming, difficult to find the right balance of things. Maybe you're one of the many silently struggling, feeling overwhelmed by the demands of degree level study, feeling confused, lacking confidence, struggling with independent study, feeling isolated, unhappy with the balance between work, rest and play, pressurised by your peers to be involved with things that aren't for you, anxious about home, feeling culture shock, experiencing anxiety about what will come following your degree in a competitive job market, wondering who you are. Some students seem to spend so much time at university consumed by worries of different kinds. If that's you, what if you could let go of the worries, engage fully with your experience and have more fun?

For others still, it's just about wanting that little bit more. Perhaps you're doing really well, your studies and the rest of life are going great, and yet there's still something missing. What could you discover if you did give it that extra something?

Whatever your experience now, the questions underlying this book are:

- How do you want your university experience to be?
  and
- What can you do to make it like that?

The phrasing of these questions is important. They place an emphasis on you.

For starters, what gets in your way? There is a whole set of ready-made answers lining up to offer a first class answer to this question. And having taught in universities for over 15 years, one of us, Will has heard them all in one form

> *Get Sorted* **is about making your university experience how you want it to be**

or another: flatmates, parents, money, illness, family, jobs, computers, other students, missing home, Facebook, lecturers, cultural differences, administrators, mobile phones, support workers, pets, alarm clocks, landlords, parties, children, sport, music, art. No doubt you can add to the list. How complete are those answers though? What excuses are they masking? What fears do they hide? Might there be things that you can do something about if you're more honest with yourself? What if you could see the point? Let go of your fears? Do away with self-doubt?

Of course those things and people are real, and of course stuff can get in the way. Alarm clock batteries can indeed run out! Things don't always work out as you plan them. And yet, you know, and we know, that different people can have very different responses to the same situation. That suggests an altogether different set of answers to the question 'what gets in your way?'

And that is where this book comes in. We invite you, challenge you even, to work out how you get in your own way, and, better still, how to take responsibility for shaping your

> **What gets in your way is often you in one form or another**

experience. This is about being honest with yourself about where you're at, what you want, your hopes, fears, dreams and ambitions. Another good bit is that you get to do this without anyone looking over your shoulder to tell you what you should do, shouldn't do or make judgements about what's right or wrong for you. Instead this is an opportunity for you to become more aware about the choices you can make and where you can take responsibility, for example with your thoughts, behaviours, actions, ambitions and even emotions (or at least your response to them).

A version of *Get Sorted* could sound like 'pull your socks up', but that's not the version we're advocating here. That implies a particular solution, a particular assumption about how you need to be. We offer a different approach in which getting sorted is about staying true to what really matters to you, with what you value and what you envision for your life, and aspiring to goals that will make a difference to your motivation and enjoyment. This means stepping past your fears and overcoming self-doubt as you draw on your inner resources for creativity, confidence, focus, relationships, and resilience.

The bottom line is that what you get from your university experience has more to do with how you approach university life than it does to all those things that are going on 'out there'. A shift in your approach can make all the difference to being how you want to be in order to make what you want

How you experience something depends on your interpretation of it

from university life. The challenge is to find the approaches that work for you, and to put them into practice. In a way the book offers you a series of ideas and strategies to experiment with to find out what works for you.

And of course what works for you will depend on you and your particular situation, and any challenges you are up against. The book is designed for you to apply the ideas to any area of your student experience and find out what will make a difference. Here we give some examples to illustrate the sorts of challenges we've found students facing.

After a few extended gap years, Bess felt she was finally studying for the degree she wanted to do – she'd changed from her original choice and postponed going to university. Somehow, though, she was finding something was lacking and she'd start questioning all over again. By working on some core foundations, Bess could rekindle a sense of why she's doing what she's doing, and making each day feel worthwhile.

Jenny was feeling stuck and under pressure. She was at the end of her second year getting high 2.2's and low 2.1's. Whatever she did, nothing seemed to make her mark higher and she was starting to feel like there was no point trying. If you are someone who finds themselves in a situation like Jenny's it might be good to explore your motivation and how to set goals that will feel worthwhile.

Mehmood was bored. He was so disappointed by his lecturers' lack of enthusiasm and the subjects on offer, he couldn't find any focus and found himself procrastinating on Facebook and gaming. He realised his results were falling short of what he wanted. There are times when we really need to refocus and find ways to manage distractions.

Chun was lacking confidence and finding it difficult adjusting to being in a new country. Whether with friends, her football team or in tutorials, she never felt what she had to say was of value and instead kept quiet and felt trapped in a shell. That was true in her studies too where she never felt she gave it her all for fear of looking stupid. There are strategies to work on building your confidence that can be applied to a range of situations.

Anna had set up the summer of her life for her second year. It was going to involve working abroad and then some travelling with a group of new friends. The problem is she hadn't realised that she also really needed to use that time to work on her dissertation. She felt a little stuck in how to find a way through. Sometimes you need to let yourself get creative to find out what might be possible.

Samantha was having the time of her life and managing to do fine in her degree. Her parents, though, had different ideas, and she felt under constant pressure to justify what she was doing. It was really getting her down and living at home wasn't helping. Relationships can be worth looking at in different ways to see what can be done differently.

Pete was overwhelmed. He was struggling with finding ways to balance his degree with his role in the student union. Even though both were going well, and he was excited by them, he realised he had little time to relax and have fun and, when he tried, he always felt guilty. He found his energy was diminishing. Resilience is something that can be built up over time, and can also diminish if we don't pay attention to ourselves.

Aakash felt broke. He had two part-time jobs, struggled to keep up with the demands of his degree, and felt anxious about his future. This wasn't a nice feeling. He found he was often getting ill and missing shifts or lectures and worrying about what he had to do next. Sometimes it's important to pause, look afresh at the situation and allow yourself to be in the here and now.

Getting sorted isn't specifically about degree performance, or employability or career or about health and well-being. It could be any one or all of these, or indeed something different. How you choose to apply the ideas in this book to get sorted is down to you. Any of the chapters could be applied to a range of situations that crop up in university life, from your studies to friends and relationships, career and health and well-being.

Part I of this book shows you how to establish your core foundations. By putting these foundations into place each day you have a platform for building the university experience you want every day. This includes being aware of your vision in life, knowing your values, noticing any 'Gremlin voices', checking in with how you are, and then choosing how you want to be... **Don't let your day start without you** It's a bit like a SatNav that calibrates itself and establishes its starting position before beginning the journey. Only once this is done can it pick the best route, avoid jams, make corrections and ultimately navigate a desired way forwards.

The following chapters in **Part II** then pick up different themes around being motivated, being focused, being confident, being creative, being in relationships and being resilient. These chapters are in no particular order, and to engage with them you need to have worked through Part I first. You can apply any of these chapters to any area of your degree life, ranging from approaching your studies (including lectures, group work, essays, exams), to your university experience as a whole (including making friends, joining societies, being in a new culture, relationships, homesickness, and balancing jobs and study), as well as to questions about the future and employability.

A final chapter offers some additional resources for enjoying the journey. It's written for when things are not quite how you'd like them to be, despite your efforts to change them. It introduces some mindfulness exercises to enable you to engage with 'what is'. This can enhance other aspects of the book while also introducing something new.

While we don't advocate a specific focus on employability and prefer to emphasise living a life you value, the other one of us, Jeff, in his work with businesses and graduate entrepreneurs has noticed how employers are increasingly saying that they want graduates who know their values, who know what they stand for, who know their strengths and who can take responsibility for their approach to life and work. Specific skills or knowledge can then be gained on the job. This book, then, not only gives you resources for living the life you want now, it may well lead to surprising results for your future ...

A note about reading this book

Get Sorted is not only about reflection. A key point about this book is that you can't just read about it, you need to do something. However much you read about running a marathon, you won't get any closer if you don't start training! Throughout the book, the chapters point to key exercises from which you'll identify key actions – these exercises are like experiments, a way to try something out, experience it, see what works and what doesn't. These are marked by the following symbol:

• Each chapter offers some key questions to reflect on, marked by a giant Q. These are questions that you can carry with you, to reflect on over time rather than answer immediately.

Any particular theme we discuss may, for you, be closely related to another theme elsewhere in the book. Where you see the symbol, we invite you to review other parts of the book:

One particular recurring theme is a bit of a pest – the Gremlin. Section 1.3 describes Gremlins in more depth. They could jump out at any point; however, there are particular moments when we think it's useful for you to be more wary. These are marked by the Gremlin symbol:

Sometimes using metaphor can be a really helpful way to capture what you're experiencing and what you would like to be experiencing. The chapters in Part II offer you a chance to think of a metaphor for your experience. These are marked by a large M:

Finally, the examples of student experience we give to illustrate how you might apply the ideas in this book all use fictitious names. However, they are real examples, written in students' own words and only edited for typos and anonymity.

Foundations

1

Foundations

Get sorted, now and every day...

'How was your day?' A simple question, one you probably ask your friends, flatmates, partners, parents and others habitually. And their responses are probably habitual too: 'fine', 'grhrrrrr', 'alright', 'awful', 'great', or simply 'don't ask'. While you might often say to a friend 'have a nice day' or 'I hope you have a great day', what if you turn this completely on its head, and ask at the start of the day 'How do you want your day to be?' As a habit.

- How would you like each day to be?
- What do you want each day to say about you?
- How do you want to be each day?

The chapters in Part II will go some way to helping you do just that. Imagine if you could start each day reminding yourself why the day matters to you and what's really important about it. A day with purpose and intention. A day when you can see how what you're doing fits in with your vision of what you want, where you're going and who you want to be. A day in which how you're being and what you're doing feels meaningful because it's connected to the things you hold dear in your life, your values. And a day in which you've put aside any irritating voices that hold you back through fear or pressure with words like 'you can't', 'you shouldn't', 'you're not good enough', 'you should be doing more'. How might that change your day?

Indeed, to take this one step further, what if you also ask, 'How am I going to approach today, whatever happens?' It's sometimes difficult to see that you have a choice in how you approach something, but you do. This is something we'll be returning to at various times in the book. However, for now, we just want to emphasise the point that you can decide how you want to be. This point is well made by Victor Frankl, a survivor of the concentration camps during the Second World War. He wrote, based on his experience in these camps, "everything can be taken from a man [or woman] but one thing: the last of the human freedoms – to choose one's attitude in any given set of circumstances, to choose one's own way" (1963, p. 104). In other words, whatever happens, you can still choose your way, your approach to a situation.

But … Yes, we know there are 'buts' lining up to make their point here. Stuff happens, and at first sight good, bad or indifferent days can seem **Whatever happens in the day, you can choose your approach** more to do with what happens to you than anything you're responsible for. For example, when things go wrong, some lectures (or lecturers) are boring, friends are demanding, parents annoying, topics uninspiring, essay deadlines overlooked, you've run out of money, it's all too difficult, you've run out of steam! And things get complicated. You're just getting down to some reading when a Facebook message pops up inviting you to a BBQ that afternoon. How do you respond? Relief to have an excuse to get away from your studies? Excitement at meeting new people? Confusion, wanting to go but feeling you ought not? A sense of pressure to socialise when you'd rather be alone? All manner of responses are possible, as they are to any given situation. In fact there can seem so many factors, so many 'buts', that can influence the answer to how you are each day and to what you achieve.

We recognise these buts. We've heard students use many of them during workshops and coaching sessions. Our point is not to say you can create anything you want to. No-one has that much power! What you can do though is start to choose how you want to be with what's around you, both the things that happen to you as well as the things you do create. How you approach the world around you – how you approach each day –

is something that, with increased awareness, can become a choice.

This is where the next few chapters come in, inviting you to set out your core foundations and use them to create the perfect day! We like to think of this a bit like a SatNav that you can tune into before you set out each day. Just like a SatNav that when you switch it on aligns itself to the orbiting satellites and then works out the best way to get you to where you want to go, we invite you to align yourself with the elements of your core foundations at the start of each day, and use them to set out your approach to the day ahead, both in what you want to do and how you want to be.

In summary, you can get sorted by starting the day as you mean to go on. Undoubtedly, you have a plan (if not see Chapter 3) and you know some of what to expect, and for sure there will be unexpected changes, surprises and pitfalls. Only now, whatever your day throws before you, you'll be in a position to be aware of what matters to you and how you can choose your way in what you do and how you approach it.

Part I offers you a way of doing this, based on four foundations:

- Making each day relevant – bring your vision to life
- Making each day meaningful – living your values
- Making each day Gremlin free – don't let them have the last word
- How are you today, really? Being aware of your starting point

Bringing these four foundations together, the final section shows how to say 'yes' to your day, every day.

Students say university days can be...

... dull as dishwater ... like a rollercoaster ...pulled in different directions ... intense ... unstructured ... hanging around ... uncertain ... like a long flight ... bombarding the senses

Students have described the perfect day as...

... fun with focus ... like climbing a mountain range ...being in the rhythm ... going with the flow ... like a carnival ... feeling accomplished

What's it like when things don't go as you want?
What's it like when you have the perfect day?

1.1 Making each day relevant – bring your vision to life!

Do you ever find yourself wondering 'What's the point?' and then maybe feeling you can't be bothered, even though you feel you must do something? Or perhaps you're really driven and getting stuff done, heading for a first-class degree, and yet in the background you're wondering (or have forgotten to ask!) 'But where does all this lead' or 'For the sake of what'? We've heard many a student say 'Where's it all leading?' or 'What's this seminar got to

- How would having a clearer vision help you each day?
- What gets in the way of dreaming the impossible?
- How honest are you being about what you really want?

do with anything?' or, 'What has this degree got to do with anything that matters in the world?' Or even a very different version, 'Just tell me what to do to get a first, I'm not bothered about the wider stuff'.

Sometimes it's worth taking a step back to ask 'What's the point?' for you. This can be really important for those needing to find some renewed motivation, and it can also be important for those of you who perhaps need to strike a better balance. Stepping back can mean finding the relevance of daily activities, lectures, studying, socialising, volunteering, leisure, paid work, or caring for someone into the context of your bigger vision of life. After all, you've made a big personal investment in this university experience, so what's the point for you? What's the purpose beyond the 'result'?

The answer can be found in building your vision. Knowing what it's all for and where it's all heading in the grander scheme of things can make all the difference to how you are now, it makes each day, each moment relevant. As Jon Kabat-Zinn writes, 'to achieve peace of mind, people have to kindle a vision of what they really want for themselves and keep that vision alive in the face of inner and outer hardships, obstacles, and setbacks' (2004, pp. 45–46).

The power of keeping hold of your vision lies in how it translates into what you do now, how you conduct your everyday moments. Keeping hold of your vision can help you deal with the things you

> A vision is neither right nor wrong, it's something to keep evolving

find hard. It can help you re-orientate your energy when you find yourself off track. Your vision can help you keep everything in proportion. It can help you feel motivated to go that extra mile. Sometimes it can be about reminding yourself of the importance of your degree to the bigger picture of what you want. And sometimes it can be about reminding yourself to keep the degree in the right perspective within the bigger picture.

For some of you an element of self-doubt may already have jumped in. You don't have a vision. What sort of commitment might a vision involve? Most visions are unrealistic. What's the point? What will people think of my vision? What if it's 'wrong'? I ought to want this, but I feel this … Our tip here is to let go and experiment at this point. You can play around with ideas, explore what different visions feel like for you. There's no right, or wrong. And, you get to change it as you learn more about yourself. What's important though, is to make sure that, in thinking about your vision, it's just that, yours. It's not a vision that you think you should have or one that you think others expect of you. It's your vision based on what matters to you.

How to experiment with your vision

There are lots of ways to think about vision and here we offer a variety of ways because some will appeal more to some than to others. It's important to recognise that defining a vision is an ongoing process and it can be revealing to revisit these exercises overtime. Creating a picture and/or writing down your vision can be an important part of the process of refining it.

Step 1 – Different ways to create a vision

Your 80th Birthday Celebration…

Imagine it's your 80th Birthday celebration. Bring the image alive: Who's there with you? What are you wearing? What do people call you? What are you doing with your life at this point in the future? How are you feeling? What have you achieved? Where are you? What are you like as a person? Now, someone who knows you well is giving a speech about you, who you are, what you've done, how you are in the world. What do they say?

Imagining your future ...

Create a timeline that marks out now and sometime into the future. Move slowly along your timeline, letting the weeks, months and years pass by until you reach a point several years ahead. Imagine here that you're experiencing a future you'd like, one you fantasise about. Ask: What have I got here? What am I doing with my life? How am I feeling? What have I achieved? Where am I? Who am I with? What am I like as a person? How do others describe me?

Tip: using objects to mark out your timeline can work well for this, for example a series of trees, park benches or pictures in a gallery. Moving physically creates a more powerful experience than imagination alone.

Picturing your vision

Following either or both of the above exercises let an image come to mind that captures your vision. This doesn't have to mean anything to anyone else. Let your imagination loose. A picture speaks a thousand words, and thinking in pictures uses different and more creative parts of our brains. This is a neat way of summarising and reminding yourself without the need for lots of words.

Tip: drawing a picture, or finding pictures that represent it, can help clarify your vision. Some people make 'picture boards' that build up over time.

60 seconds to speak to the world

Imagine you have 60 seconds on a stage and the whole world is listening. What would you say?

Tweet the world

If you could write one tweet the whole world would read, what would you tweet?

Step 2 – Clarify your vision (for now)

Building on the previous exercises have a go at capturing your vision in ten words, or as a picture if you prefer, in a way that's meaningful for you.

Complete the following sentence:

My vision is _____ _____ _____ _____ _____ _____

Remember, in developing your vision, this is something to keep coming back to. It's not set in stone, you can change it as you learn more about yourself and as life moves forwards. For now, gaining more clarity about your vision is the job in hand.

Also remember your vision doesn't have to feel 'realistic'. Visions can create surprising results. There are many people in history who've had what at the time seemed 'unrealistic' visions which they kept alive. Visions of peace, of justice, of care for nature, of travelling to space, of running a mile in under 4 minutes. And yet some of those visions came true: establishing women's voting rights, ending apartheid in South Africa, landing a person on the moon, personal computing, running a mile in less than 4 minutes, global communications networks, the end of the cold war .... So what if your vision is grander than feels possible? Does a child who fantasises about becoming a world cup footballer lose out by treasuring such a vision? Or does she gain from learning about fitness, skill, focus, dedication, team work?

Examples of students' visions

My vision is to make a positive contribution to the world

My vision is to be the best I can at whatever I do

My vision is to offer care and compassion to people I love

My vision is to relax and enjoy what life has to offer

My vision is to live life as a pomegranate

My vision is to inspire other people with disabilities to break boundaries

My vision is to establish myself in a solid career

My vision is to treat life as one long adventure

My vision is to address injustice in my country

My vision is to be at peace with myself and others

My vision is to feel part of the community

My vision is to honour each and every moment of life

My vision is to live in harmony with nature

1.2 Making each day meaningful – living your values

A vision provides a handy foundation to check in with each day, giving purpose and direction to what you're doing. Sometimes, though, it can be hard to relate that bigger picture to what you're actually doing. If your vision is about being at peace with yourself, how does that relate to feeling bored by the prospect of five lectures on a cold winter's day? If your vision is to do with developing your career, what does that have to do with sitting at the supermarket checkout for on an eight-hour shift? If your vision is about making life an adventure, perhaps that seems far away from slaving over a 3000-word essay?

- What do you really value?
- What gets in the way of living your values?
- What do your values say about you?

The step we ask you to take now is from vision to values. Knowing your values is like having an internal guidance system that shines a light on what's really important to you. Your values can guide you in what decisions to make, in what you stand for, in how you want to be. Your values are based on what really matters to you, they make you who you are. It's not surprising then that when you stay true to your values you'll feel good about yourself, and when you don't, you'll feel like something is wrong or missing.

Each moment is an opportunity to be true to your values

ONE SMALL STEP FOR VALUES

ONE GIANT LEAP FOR YOU

How to discover and live your values

It's not always easy to name what you value. By reflecting on significant 'peak' and 'trough' experiences in your life you can start to identify what's important to you, that is, your values. You can build up words, or phrases that capture something for you. With key values identified, you can then look at which are the most important to you and how well you're living those values each day. A small change can make all the difference.

Step 1 – Finding your values

First, think of a specific time when things were just right. It might be recent or some years ago. In coaching sessions students have used all sorts of 'peak' experiences. Sometimes people identify a particular moment when they passed an exam, or a time when they felt on top of their sport, or a time when they felt deeply connected to other people. Others choose an example from a previous job when they felt in the flow. It's about a moment when you felt good and on a roll; ignore whatever happened next. Re-live that peak moment vividly in as much detail as possible. Where were you? Who were you with? How were you feeling? What could you see? What could you hear? What were you doing? What sensations did you feel in your body? What would somebody watching you have seen? Now think about what really mattered to you in that moment. What made everything feel just right? What was important to you? Write down key words that describe this.

Second, now the opposite: think of a specific time when things weren't right, a trough, when things felt wrong! A moment when you felt angry, wound up, frustrated, annoyed or upset. It might be recent or some years ago. Perhaps something someone said or did, something you heard about or witnessed first-hand, something that wound you up. Choose a moment that you can remember vividly and re-live it in detail. Where were you? Who were you with? How were you feeling? What could you see? What could you hear? What were you doing? What sensations did you feel in your body? What was going on? What made you so angry, frustrated, annoyed or upset? What was important to you in that moment that was being challenged, suppressed or violated? Write down key words that capture this.

The list of words you're generating are a window on your values, things that really matter to you. You can build on these, they're not fixed. To explore them further other questions that help to get to your values are: Where do I love to be? What do I love doing? Who do I enjoying being with? Who inspires me? Who annoys me? What makes me angry about the world? What do I appreciate about life? Sometimes it can be insightful just to ask yourself, repeatedly, 'what's important?', over and over again for about 5 minutes to see where it takes you.

Note: it's OK if some values contradict each other. You may have a set of values about solitude and time for reflection, and a set of values about socialising and community. The good news is: you can have both although perhaps not honour them both at the same time, but over time you can find the right balance.

Step 2 – Clustering your values

It's not surprising that something as important as values may not easily fit into simple words. Some of your words may overlap. You can start to connect words up and perhaps a new word will appear that captures them? Perhaps you need to make up a phrase to join some together? The important thing is that the words capture what's important to you. Aim to create a core list of between seven and ten values.

Step 3 – The most important values

Taking your list of seven to ten core values, how would you rank them in terms of importance to you? This can be a useful exercise in teasing out what really does matter. Rank them: which is the most important, which the least?

Tip: you could imagine you're in a hot air balloon. You're descending too quickly and will soon crash into the ground. To ascend you need to throw out two of your values. Which would you let go of? Which would you keep?

Step 4 – Living your values

How well are you living these values during your university experience? Give each of your values a score between 1 and 10. A score of 1 means you're hardly honouring or staying true to that value at the moment. A score of 10 means that you're fully living that value.

Value	Rank	Living it
Fun-Adventure	3	4/10
Being at my best	2	3/10
Peaceful-Alone	6	7/10
Caring for others	5	6/10
etc.	etc.	etc.

Step 5 – one small step for values, one giant leap for you!

You have a list of values and how much they mean to you as well as a sense, a score, of the extent to which, during your university experience, you're staying true to your values. Pick one value for which you would like to improve the score. Think of what that value means to you. How could you approach the day ahead in a way that will improve that score? Don't put it off! Today, this day, what small step, however small, could you take towards improving that score for that value in your university experience? We dare you to give it a go … And note, by university experience we mean this in a holistic sense – it might be, for example, that booking yourself in for some kind of exercise would be part of improving the experience by honouring a value of health, or making contact with someone at home who's not well would be honouring a value of family.

Tip: when faced with a decision or a lack of motivation or when just feeling in the wrong mood, remind yourself of your values and what value you want to live up to. Being aware of your values in this way will be a learning process.

Some words that might capture your values …

Harmony	Family	Dynamism
Solitude	Joy	Tradition
Sustainability	Growth	Freedom to choose
Accomplishment	Fortitude	Presence
Resilience	Beauty	Being understood
Trust	Understanding	Spirituality
Peace	Kindness	Authenticity
Independence	Style	Supporting
Community	Empathy	Empowerment
Fun	Acknowledgement	Good speech
Elegance	Order	Integrity
Connection	Recognition	Achievement
Cooperation	Vitality	The outdoors
Love	Being on the edge	Nurturing
Risk taking	Honesty	Excellence
Aesthetics	Prosperity	Commitment

Student experience – Simon

Sometimes when you're feeling unsure or uncertain, reflecting on your values can be a powerful way of seeing different possibilities. Simon used this in thinking about possible careers:

"Coming up to my final exams I began to reflect whether, throughout university, I had achieved what I had set out to do (get a degree in something I enjoyed, meet people, to have a good time) and whether this had made me feel fulfilled. I was also applying for jobs, which made me reassess what

I wanted to do after university. I was feeling disheartened and frustrated as I had continually been applying for jobs since the beginning of third year and yet had got nothing, which in turn made me anxious as to what the future may hold. I was also discouraged by the fact that I had done a degree which I really enjoyed, yet was so far, unsuccessful in obtaining a job relating to it, or other graduate jobs for that matter. I took some time out of writing multiple pieces of coursework, just to sit quietly and think; to have the chance to listen to the birds in the garden and ponder and contemplate whilst staring out the window. (I would have preferred to do this outside, but typical Yorkshire weather, it was raining!). Instead of writing a lot down I just pictured the moment when things were just so, as it was nice to remember. Yet when thinking about a trough experience I felt compelled to write things down, in order to get the feelings of frustration and anger out. Ranking my core values wasn't easy as I felt they were all important, yet thinking about which ones you would let go if you really had to (the hot air-balloon scenario) made this easier. I realised that when things are not just so, I tend to move on and not really think about it, but through reflecting on my values I can now see where the feelings experienced in the trough situation came from and consequently overcome them. I also realised that perhaps I am too hard on myself sometimes and when I am tied up in making the people around me happy that I tend to forget the things that matter to me and what I value. When choosing what jobs to apply for and future plans, I began to think more about what I value – understanding, growth, trust, which in turn will hopefully lead to fulfilment in the future. It allowed me to feel more positively about the future, to move on from feeling frustrated and disheartened, to look at what I truly value and the things in life which are important to me. I am less worried over the uncertainty of the future and have made numerous plans and have looked at my options as to what to do when I finish university. I may go onto further study as it is something which I enjoy and really value. The experience now is full of hope."

1.3 Making your day Gremlin-free – don't let them have the last word

Some of you may not yet be convinced by what we've suggested so far. You may be reading on, not really trying out the exercises. That's your choice and we're not going to try and persuade you. This isn't an academic book, we're not trying to argue anything. We are not even trying to be right. Indeed, there's no way to be right. Rather, what we suggest is it's worth trying things out to see what works for you.

- What holds you back?
- How do you feel when you listen to your Gremlins?
- How do you get in your own way?

So, what stops you from … having a go … trying something out … taking a risk … being playful … exploring something new … asking questions …. being at your best … going first … sharing … contributing …. saying what you really think … experimenting … relaxing …. being you…having fun…? Who has the last word on all this? And, what might stop you trying out the experiments offered in this book or exploring this chapter?

Think for a moment: how often do you hear yourself saying 'but', 'can't', 'ought', 'should', 'not good enough', 'shouldn't', 'must', 'mustn't', 'ought not'? How often do these voices in your head hold you back? People have called this voice many things, including the 'Inner Critic' (Melanie Greene, 2008), the Gremlin (Rick Carson, 2003), Self 1 (Timothy Gallwey, 1974), the Demon (Steve Peters, 2012), the Saboteur (Henry Kimsey-House et al., 2011). It's that voice that interrupts what you're doing, knocks your confidence, says you need to be doing something else, says it will never work, says you should have done better, says you're not up to it or that you'll never be good enough or even that you must be the best at it, whatever the cost. The voice comes in all shapes and forms and can sometimes be really loud, persistent and particularly annoying.

Gremlins raise the stakes so that everything matters

There are times while at university when the Gremlin voice really dominates and loves to have the last word when something goes wrong … 'I told you so!' Perhaps some critical feedback or exam results that weren't as you'd hoped they would be. On the other hand it often jumps out at you just when you thought things were going well, raising all kinds of self-doubt. Sometimes trying to stop you ('What's the point?'), sometimes trying to push you harder ('You're not fast enough') and always unhelpful! Always throwing rocks in your way despite a smooth path ahead. What it tends to say often leaves you feeling disempowered and without many choices. It tells you what the situation is and why you either 'must' do *X* or 'can't' do *Y*. Indeed, Gremlins like to raise the stakes so that everything matters – if you 'don't' or 'can't' or 'won't' then everything is over!

Before we go any further, please note that while your Gremlins often masquerade as if they're the voice of another, don't be fooled! Your Gremlins aren't real people. When students have started to think about their Gremlins we've heard them say things like 'Oh, I know my Gremlin alright, it's my mum' or, 'It's my teacher from school that says those things'. Here's the deal: it might be the actions or words of 'real' people that initiated or now reinforce your Gremlin voice BUT, BUT, BUT the Gremlin is your own creation, it's your inner voice. It might be a voice you learnt from somebody else, but it's you and you alone that keeps it alive. In a way, then, it's made in your imagination. It doesn't belong with anyone else and, as you'll see, it can be brought under your management.

How to notice and manage your Gremlins

The principle with Gremlins is that if you can learn to spot them, you can make a step towards stopping your automatic response to them. By naming them and capturing what they typically say, you can start to spot them more easily. There are also things you can do to manage them when they still hang around. Acknowledging them, rather than just hoping they'll go away, is a big part of this.

Step 1 – Gremlin Spotting

Over the next few days, pay attention to when your inner voice is using Gremlin-type words (ought, should, shouldn't, must, must not, can't). For example, 'You don't know enough about that topic', 'You ought to have done more reading', 'You shouldn't risk writing anything wrong', 'You're not working hard enough', 'You should be with your friends'. Also, notice how that voice tends to generalise, raising the stakes to be all or nothing: 'Get this wrong and it's all over', 'It's all too much, I can't do anything anymore', 'My degree is a disaster', 'Don't make a mistake here', 'Change is too scary, be careful', 'I'm always a failure'.

Name your Gremlin voices. Some people call them 'John' or 'Harry', others name them based on what they're saying, 'Hedge your bets', 'Mr Risk Averse', others use cartoon characters or characters from novels – whatever works for you so that you've a shorthand. What do your Gremlins look like? Draw a picture!

Spend time identifying the consequence of your Gremlins in relation to what you do (or don't do) and how you feel. You can do this by completing the following:

- My Gremlin is called ....
- He, she, it ... is very fond of saying ....
- The consequence is that I ......

Step 2 – Starting to manage your Gremlins

You could stick with your Gremlins if you want to. After all you've had them for some time and you're doing a degree, so that's pretty good going. So why bother to free yourself of them now? You might find it helpful to know that one of the nice things about Gremlins is that they're very loyal; however harshly you treat them they're always willing to come back! What follows then are like a series of experiments to see what works for you, knowing that if they don't work, nothing will be lost.

Daily Gremlin spotting

You can be as creative with this as you like in a way that works for you. For example, if you've identified ten Gremlins write out ten pages with all ten listed on each one. Whenever you spot a Gremlin, cross it off the list and throw that page in the bin as a way of saying good bye. You have ten pages. See if you can spot all ten Gremlins in one day. Or over the course of a week.

Depowering Gremlins

This is a menu of choices and no doubt some will work for you and some won't, so feel free to add your own. Imagine your Gremlin as vividly as possible. What colour is it? Try changing it to something else. Try different colours until it feels different. Try different patterns over it: perhaps something stripy, something ridiculous? How loud is the Gremlin? Change the volume, does that help? Change the tone, what happens?

A squeaky voice perhaps? How big is the Gremlin? Change the size, what happens? How close to you is the Gremlin? What happens if it moves further and further away, until it's more distant? … Keep trying different things that change its form in a way that, for you, depowers it.

When they dig in their heels

Every now and then the Gremlin really digs in its heels. It's worth checking something here. Is there some truth you need to acknowledge? Is there something the Gremlin is saying that you need to listen to? Could there be a way of reframing the voice from 'ought' to 'want'? … Might that lead to a more useful feeling and better set of actions?

Note: It can take time to get more skilled at managing your Gremlins, and of course the more skilled you are, the more crafty those Gremlins may get. So it's important to keep working on this. When faced with a decision (not) to do something you can now double check: How loud is my Gremlin?, What self-limiting assumptions am I imposing? What's at stake?

Student experience – Anna

Finding creative ways to visualise your Gremlins can create surprising metaphors for how you might manage them. Anna came up with a way to imagine training them:

"I was feeling very stressed over the amount of work that I had to do and the time-frame in which I had to do it, as well as the quality of the work that I was producing. It didn't matter that I had always previously got my work in on time, or that my marked work came back at an acceptable level, I was still scared that I was going to do terribly or that I wouldn't be able to get it in by the deadline. The stress and the pressure that I was putting myself under to get work done and get it done well was stopping me from enjoying and getting the most out of the work that I was doing and what I was learning. It meant that I was spending most of my time at uni stuck in the library stressed about how I wasn't doing enough.

For me, it helped to visualise each thought/gremlin as an annoying, yappy, ill-trained Chihuahua that needed to be socialised and trained as outside of university I spend quite a bit of time with dogs. Just as gremlins only want the best for you but don't quite know the correct way to go about it, so dogs generally want to please and be with you but can end up being over-zealous and out of control.

I then named my first Chihuahua/Gremlin Jaan and he is very fond of saying that there isn't enough time to do all the work that needs to be done. The second Chihuahua/Gremlin I called Steve. He is very fond of telling me that

I should do better at my work.

Next I visualised how I would get the Chihuahuas to behave, not by getting really cross, shouting at them and shutting them out (ignoring them) like I had when they were just random thoughts, but by telling them to calm down, telling them that I was in charge and I know what I was doing and whenever they started barking again I would repeat the process.

Part of this process was getting them to stay where I told them to stay rather than bothering me constantly and stopping me from working, firstly beside my chair or under the desk, building up to leaving them outside. This was something I visualised each time I started working, whether this was in the library or at home.

With my Chihuahuas calm I was able to acknowledge that actually I had always got my work in on time and that it was good enough. This meant that I could relax a bit on both counts and the grades on the work I've handed in since I learnt to control my Gremlins has been better than before. This has given me more confidence in telling the Chihuahuas that they don't constantly need to be barking at me. Getting good marks back has also made me feel more competent and given me more confidence as a result.

Writing essays is far less stressful now than it used to be and whenever the Gremlins do become overly noisy again I'm able to spot them and get them back under control easily. I am also able to recognise Gremlins in other areas of my life and socialise them into less unruly behaviour."

Gremlins that students have described

'Doubt' is very fond of saying 'You're not (doing) good enough' and the impact it has on me is I feel pretty useless and that I don't have anything particularly useful/helpful to contribute to a discussion

'Jaan' is very fond of saying 'There isn't enough time to do all the work that needs to be done.' The consequence is that I end up feeling very stressed, with heavy pressure to complete work.

'Dragon Face' is very fond of saying that 'You could have done better and worked harder.' The impact this has on me is that I expect too much of myself, so find it hard to switch off and do nothing.

'Blobby' is very fond of telling me 'You should do better at whatever it is you're attempting to do (e.g., sports/work).' The consequence of this is that I often feel as if I have let myself down, even when I have done quite well.

'Kate' is very fond of saying 'You shouldn't draw so much attention to yourself, asking/answering questions or asking for help.' The consequence of this is that I spend a lot of time second-guessing my motives for doing so.

'Mrs Mop' is fond of telling me 'You are responsible for how other people feel and you need to look after them.' As a consequence I tend to feel overly anxious about hurting people and to berate myself heavily when I do, even if it is something minor.

'Squadron Leader' is fond of saying 'You are being pathetic. Everyone goes through bad things, most of it much worse than yours, and they don't make nearly as much fuss about it.' As a consequence I feel unsure about whether I am over-reacting to my situation and question why I am making such a big deal out of it.

'Control freak' tends to say 'You should make sure it's all planned out before you do anything at all.' The consequence is I spend time mapping everything out and avoiding doing what's in front of me; often re-planning, writing more to-do lists, just to make sure.

1.4   How are you today, really? Being aware of your starting point

Sometimes your day unravels before you've even got started. You've got a splitting headache from reading *Get Sorted* too late the night before, you're feeling emotionally drained after a friend poured their soul out to you on the phone, your back is seized up from watching a film on an uncomfortable old sofa, you find yourself distracted by an exciting job opportunity. And yet, in seeking the perfect day, you ignore all that and you set out with all the best intentions for your studies, planning to go to the gym, to get together with your friends, spend time looking into your career, make contact with home or whatever else you'd love to get done that day and ... it just isn't happening. It's as if you're trying to walk the wrong way up an escalator.

- What do you learn from noticing how you really are?
- How could you be more considerate to yourself?
- What are you ignoring as you set out on your day?

   We suggest part of creating the perfect day needs to involve asking a very simple question: 'How am I today'? When you ask a friend 'How are you?', you probably do so out of courtesy. You'd probably answer with courtesy too. 'Fine thanks, and you?' Or perhaps, 'Really good, how are you?' Or 'Not too bad, how about you?' Or 'Alright'. In asking yourself, 'How am I?' you'll need to put courtesy aside and allow yourself to be honest. Each day brings different experiences in your thoughts, emotions and body. Perhaps you're tired, anxious, excited, pessimistic, optimistic, sad, happy, hot, cold, a complex bundle of all sorts of things. Just a few

Start the day from where you are

moments spent checking-in with yourself can really help in setting you up for the day. Knowing where you are at the start of the day will help in working out what's sensible to set out to do, in how you might adjust your expectations of yourself, as well as for working out what else you might need to pay attention to. To look forwards to the day, you need to know where you are now. It's part of the SatNav calibrating itself for its current position.

How to notice how you (really) are

In a way this is the most straight forward of our 'how to' exercises and yet in some ways it can be the most challenging. We often walk around unaware of how we are feeling emotionally, what our thoughts are doing, and what our body needs. The principle here is to spend a few moments asking yourself just that: What are my thoughts doing? How am I emotionally? How is my body? You can then adjust your expectations as well as pay attention to something if you need to.

First, how are you in your body? What sensations are you experiencing? Sore, hot, cold, strong, weak, achy, stiff, twitchy, tense, relaxed, loose, energised, restless, heavy, light? Sometimes it can be hard to know. Try noticing your breathing as a starting point for being in touch with what your body is feeling.

Second, what thoughts can you notice that are already in your head? Try imagining standing back and watching them, like a cat trying to spot a mouse come out of the mouse-hole.

Third, how are you feeling emotionally? Are you happy, sad, angry, excited, hurt, guilt-ridden, anxious, expectant? How's your outlook? Pessimistic, optimistic, nonplussed?

At this point you may see some links between how you are in your body, your thoughts and your emotions about the day.

Tip: some people find it helpful to keep a note of how they are over time, a mood map, to see if any patterns emerge. For the moment though, we want you to focus on, well, this moment. Given how you are in this moment, what feels right for you to do today? Where do you need to pay attention?

1.5 Making it happen – saying 'Yes' to your day

This chapter brings together the four foundations of Part I. This is where you bring together the different elements of your Vision, Values, Gremlins and Awareness to set out what you want to do each day and how you're going to approach it. It's the moment where you switch on your SatNav to calibrate itself to the orbiting satellites and then work out the best route for the day – including

- What does your approach to your day say about you?
- Who or what do you let take charge of your mood?
- What will you gain by committing to what's important to you?

looking for any traffic alerts and potential hotspots. Your SATNAV calibrates your vision, your values, your Gremlins, and how you are as you set out your goals for the day. This SatNav is like an internal guide that enables you to set out how you want to approach the day, from within.

 Saying yes to your day

The principle here is to ask yourself a series of questions that will set up how you want to approach the day ahead. These questions invite you to see how each day is part of your vision and your values, how Gremlins might get in the way, and the importance of being aware of how you are. The questions ask you what you're committing to in terms of how you want to be for the day i.e. what you're saying yes to.

Before you start your day, take a moment to try the following. A few minutes is all you need and it can make the world of difference to your whole day.

First, notice how you are, emotionally, physically, outlook. Acknowledge your starting point.

Second, spot any Gremlins that may be lurking – you might find one or two, or a few, lined up waiting to interfere with your day (and maybe none, great!). Notice them, perhaps say 'Good morning!' and do any tricks that you've found from Section 1.3 to help manage them.

Third, thinking about your day ahead, what values will you be honouring as you carry out your day? Remember, often when faced with something you don't like doing but which is necessary, it can be useful to realise how doing it is all part of your wider values and your vision.

Fourth, remembering your vision, how does what you're doing connect to your bigger picture?

Finally, how are you going to approach the day ahead? To help answer the question you can think about what you're committing to in your day. What are you saying 'yes' to and what are you saying 'no' to? These two words are immensely powerful. Think of your degree – or an aspect of it like reading, essay writing, lab work, exams, revision – and say 'No, No, No' a few times. How do you feel? Now think of the same thing and say 'Yes, Yes, Yes' a few times. See what difference you notice. Saying yes and saying no feel different, they create a different way of being with things. In answering the question, 'How are you going to approach the day ahead?', identify three things you're saying 'yes' to and three things you're saying 'no' to.

Tip: if you're having trouble identifying what to say 'yes' to then try saying 'no' to three things first and then identify what that means you are saying yes to, for example 'No to feeling anxious about my essay' might become 'Yes to being calm while I write'. Or 'No to the weight of thinking about my future' might become 'Yes to a sense of lightness and focus on what I'm doing now'.

Note, it can be hard to know what to commit to when you're feeling particularly low or frustrated. Those are the times when seeing that you have a choice can feel the hardest, and yet the very times when it can become the most helpful. Later chapters in the book will help with that.

Two additional tips here may also help:

Tip: visualising everything going well. Just like high jumpers, skiers, racing drivers, actors, musicians or sales representatives who visualise their 'success' and get into the mindset they want before they perform, you can use mental rehearsal for the daily challenges of your degree experience, i.e. imagining yourself doing something in just the way you want to do it. Imagine it going well. How do you feel? What do you see? What do you hear? What are you saying 'yes' to in that moment?

Tip: a constant reminder. To keep alive the approach they're saying 'yes' to, some students have found it helpful to have a visual or audio reminder. Students have come up with all sorts of things that work for them: cartoon characters, pictures of fun fair rides, a particular technology, ying and yang, dolphins, a bird, holiday photo, rainbow etc. They have placed this on their walls, as screen savers, as desktops, badges, on phones. The picture can provide a constant reminder, a cue to saying 'yes' to how you want to be for the day. And the same goes for music and sounds.

What you might say yes to ...

...to being clear	...to lightness	...to focus
...to being assertive	...to having fun	...to achieving my goals
...to being a good friend	...to learning	...to adventure
...to security	...to engagement	...to excitement
...to calmness	...to honouring my values	...to commitment
...to health	...to not giving up	...to caring
...to vitality	...to being alive	...to laughing
...to setting my agenda	...to love	...to being motivated

Student experience – Michael

Sometimes you can lose sight of what's important to you and each day can feel like you're not sure what you are doing or why. Michael found he was really struggling to balance his university life:

"I was struggling to have a prolonged period in which I could readily put things aside, so I applied the 'Saying Yes' task to balancing my life. I was either wholly working, with very little social time, or wholly socialising, with very little working time which spiralled and made me incredibly unhappy and frustrated whilst either working or socialising.

To use the 'Saying Yes' challenge I took time out every morning to let my mind go blank, making sure that I didn't set unrealistic expectations each day, and attempting not to get worked up the night before about the work for the next day. Instead I set my aims for any day, on the day. I made myself a cup of tea and sat in the living room and noticed how I was feeling that particular day. I would work out what I thought was possible and what I thought wasn't and make a mental note. Here I would then focus on why I thought I couldn't manage a certain amount of balance. If I thought that on that particular day I would have to work on campus until 7pm then I would ask 'Why am I saying no to socialising?', and 'Why am I saying yes to doing all that work?' I would then challenge myself to say yes to something I believed would be impossible to fit into my day.

Continuing with the aforementioned situation I would instead say to myself, 'Half an hour less work will not hurt, to say yes to watching a little TV with your housemates'. From this I would realise that I wasn't just saying yes to the event but also to being happier in general. By creating a balance, rather than just finding it, I was in control of the 'yes' and in avoiding the 'no'. Vice versa, saying yes to getting work done meant that I had a sense of achievement and fulfilment. I realised that my sights were set realistically but that I needed to think about things to organise them better. This whole exercise meant that this eventually came much more naturally to me. I would not need to remind myself to think about the day ahead and saying yes, but instead when I woke up I would think about it subconsciously as I was getting dressed or lying in bed."

Part
II

Building your Resources

What gets you going?
Finding your motivation

If you were offered a prize of a jar of Marmite for the best essay, some of you might say 'yum' while others will say 'yuck'! We all have different tastes, and so too we are all motivated by different things. When you look at the diversity of students at university and what they get up to, it becomes pretty clear that people have a whole range of motivations for being there. There are those who are career-driven, those who are passionate about their studies, those who are looking for a good time, those looking to experience a new country and those who thought this was the safest thing to do for now. And so, too, when it comes down to feeling motivated in what you want to get done, what will make one person tick will be quite different to another.

- What would it mean to have more passion in what you're doing?
- How often do you make the most of your capabilities?
- What do your goals say about you?

In this chapter we turn to the often misused and misrepresented theme of 'goal setting' to look at what works for you in finding your motivation. Goal setting is something of an art. Done badly, it can lead to detrimental results. Think of the student determined to get the highest grade, to the detriment of their physical and mental health, as well as to their friendships and love of life. Or the student so focused on ensuring they get into the career they want, they lose all enjoyment of the process. Indeed, misplaced goal setting can create unhelpful anxiety. Goal setting can also lead to a feeling of underwhelm and a lack of drive. There are students who haven't found the challenge they were expecting from the study, are disappointed by the university experience as a whole, or are so unsure about the future that they can't see the point in what they're doing.

MOTIVATION = ENJOYMENT – BOREDOM

Somewhere within the space between overwhelm and underwhelm is the place that is right for you to keep you motivated. That motivation might come in different forms. It might be outcome oriented, for example getting a good mark, getting things done on time or sending off ten CVs to potential employers. The motivation might be more about process for you, for example enjoying the challenge of learning something new or rekindling some excitement about university life. Whether you find it's more about the outcome, the process, or the experience, or a combination of all of these, the sections in this chapter will allow you to test out different possibilities to find out what gets you going.

 Before even looking at how to turn your goal into action, you need to be clear on where in your university experience some goal setting could come in handy. We suggest there are three ways to think about this. The first is to look at your university experience as a whole. You can do this through the 'balance' wheels and exercises (Section 7.5). They will help you see which areas of your experience are out of balance and where attention is needed. The second is to think about how you're approaching your university experience. It may be that your 'goal' is not so much about the doing of your degree as about your confidence, focus, creativity, relationships or resilience. All of these areas can also benefit from goal setting. Of course, at the same time, setting a specific degree goal may also help in these areas. You may find that with achieving your goals your self-confidence builds. It might be that having goals in place – whether or not you achieve them – helps keep you focused and enjoying the journey. Knowing what your goals are – and which goalposts are moveable – could also be important to your resilience when you suffer the inevitable setbacks. The third is more specific. There may be a particular piece of work that you need to complete – like some writing or field work or data analysis? Perhaps a presentation you have looming over you? In all these things there are ways in which thinking about the 'goal' can help.

Where you need more motivation we invite you to explore:
- Overcoming terminal vagueness – getting clear on what you're aiming for.
- Elevating your motivation – reaching to the heart of what matters.
- Where are you setting your sights?
- Turning goals into actions – how much to stretch what you do

Students say when their motivation is low it's like ...
... wearing soggy shoes ... feeling stuck to the couch ... lethargic ... flat ... a snail ... a dark icy winter ... dense forest ... a monsoon

Students say when their motivation is high it's like ...
... a steam train rolling ... spring in each step ...COME ON!!! ... can't wait to start ... the whistle blows to start the match ... a fountain ... a summer's day ... a work of art

What's it like for you when you're not motivated?
What's it like when you're motivated?

Examples of areas for goal setting

Completing a dissertation as soon as possible

Feeling more confident about doing presentations

Developing a better relationship with my lecturers/tutors

Becoming more efficient at getting things done

Creating more 'down time'

Getting a better balance between the degree and the rest of life

Feeling good about my writing

Managing responsibilities at home

Handling criticism from lecturers/tutors

Having more fun

Taking more care of myself

Feeling more committed to the degree process

Opening up some career opportunities

Finding ways to become more creative ...

2.1   Overcoming terminal vagueness – getting clear on what you're aiming for

Making the arrangement 'I'll see you in London next week' while a bit 'hit and miss' still has its attractions. You're not pinned down, there's less commitment and more flexibility. By the same token vague goals in the shape of 'I'll do more reading over the next few months' or 'I'll start eating properly soon' or 'I'll join some societies next term' can also feel attractive. On the surface it may seem that by keeping things open ended it reduces the sense of overwhelm and makes the pressure feel more manageable. In some situations this may be just right. Reading a novel might lose the pleasure if you know you've limited time to complete it. Sometimes, however, a lack of clarity can be hiding what's really needed and, in doing so, add to the feeling of 'it's all too much'. If attracted to terminal vagueness our request is for you to be curious about the payback. What do you gain from that vagueness? And what's the cost?

Clarity can make things more manageable

    We know from experience that some students struggle when it comes to setting measurable time-bound goals. However, we've also learnt that even the most intangible pieces of work in a degree, such as creative writing processes, can be more manageable and more achievable when there's a clear goal in sight. We all have our limits: we need sleep, food and rest. And we have deadlines. What works for you is what works for you, so be creative in exploring your goal setting. Indeed, we've found students get some surprising benefits by making their goals clearer. They've found themselves less confused as they focus on what they're aiming for, less stressed as their goals feel within range, and felt more progress and achievement in knowing what completion looks like. Here we invite you to explore what greater clarity might mean for you with a 'smarter' way of setting your goals.

How to get clear on what you're aiming for

The principle here is that the more vague the goal the less motivation you'll feel, because it's hard to know whether you're on target or not. You might not even know when you've made it! We're going to use SMART goal setting as a formula for getting clarity. There are variations in the usage, however we use SMART to set goals that are Specific, Measureable, Attainable, Relevant and Time-bound. In the other sections of this chapter you can discover how to add some ART to SMART by elevating your motivation to find Resonance (Section 2.2), pushing your Aspirations by exploring what's possible (Section 2.3), and finding some Thrill by finding the right stretch (Section 2.4).

Pick a goal area that would be good to explore then make sure that your goal is stated in the positive, i.e. what you want rather than what you don't want. For example 'I don't want to feel so tired' could be stated as 'I want to feel fresh and invigorated'. Now apply the SMART formula to your goal:

1 Make it SPECIFIC. Be clear and precise about the what, who, where and which of the goal. Make it tangible.

2 Make it MEASURABLE. How will you know your goal is achieved? What evidence will you have to prove when you've done it? What will you see, hear and feel? This could be, for example, time spent doing something, chapters read, words written, number of pages in a file, number of contacts made, amount of data processed, feelings of relief or pride.

3 Make it ATTAINABLE. Is meeting your goal achievable? The whole essay in one day might be out of range, a clear introduction and conclusions might be more likely? Is the way forward clear, i.e. the 'how to' for attaining your goal? Is achieving your goal in your control or does it depend on others? For example getting a certain percentage for an essay depends on the person marking it, while aiming to do your best possible piece of work, written in a way that meets certain standards is in your control. Also, how does your goal fit with your other priorities? When you add them altogether what does attainability feel like then? Adjust your goal as needed.

4 Check for RELEVANCE. Is this the right goal for you at this time in light of your vision and other things going on for you?

5 Make it TIME-BOUND. When will you complete your goal? Be precise, what completion date and time are you aiming for? What are the timings for milestones you need to meet along the way?

Tip: to build more commitment you can share your SMART goal with a friend. And, if it feels motivating, you can also reward yourself on completion or as you reach certain milestones.

Student experience – Charlotte

Sometimes seeing the enormity of the work you have to do can make it feel like it's not worth starting. Charlotte was feeling guilty about procrastinating:

"I applied the challenge to my university work as I had been having a problem with procrastination – the more I worried about not doing work, the more I felt like it was an impossible task and didn't do work; the cycle went on. I was feeling anxious about work all the time and it was preventing me from doing other things in my life such as having a social life and committing to extracurricular activities. I used the SMART formula with the aim of 'I want to have more balance in life and feel like I have accomplished a lot each time I do work.' I already felt like it was 'specific' enough, but decided to introduce 'measurement' as 'I will have done at least three hours of revision for each subject a day and revised every day until my exams – I will feel proud of myself and know that I had done the best I possibly could.' As to 'attainability', I then rethought about my goal and readjusted it to two hours a day. I certainly felt it was 'relevant' and I brought in being 'time-bound' by telling myself that I would look over everything I had done at the end of each week so it was broken down and didn't seem an impossible task. This alone was already helpful before I added the ART technique, something which showed me that I was aiming for the right thing and for the right reasons. From this challenge I learned that I needed to break the vicious circle by making work seem less of a daunting task. Once I had figured this out I was then able to set myself smaller tasks and each time I had completed them I felt like I had accomplished something. This feeling of accomplishment made me feel more confident within myself to go and enjoy my time at university without the constant feelings of guilt that I was previously experiencing. Overall, it had a large impact on the way I live and will be living for the next couple of years. I now feel like I can achieve more in all aspects of my life."

2.2 Elevating your motivation – reaching to the heart of what matters

Do you have those moments in your degree where it's just not happening and you wonder 'what's the point?' Lectures you find boring, reading material that doesn't stimulate, essay

Getting to the heart of what matters rekindles enjoyment

topics that you can't 'get into', modules that don't inspire, friends that disappoint, difficulties at home, sports teams that are not as competitive as you like, clubs or societies you find to be very average. At times perhaps the whole university experience seems pointless. Why does any of it matter? Then what? At times like these how do you lift your motivation and re-kindle your enjoyment? One way of doing this is to re-discover what it is about your goals that makes them important to you, i.e. to ask, why do they matter in the first place.

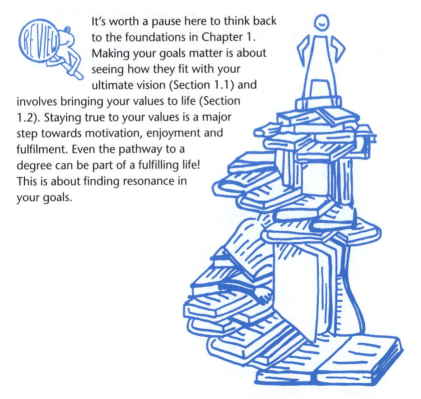

It's worth a pause here to think back to the foundations in Chapter 1. Making your goals matter is about seeing how they fit with your ultimate vision (Section 1.1) and involves bringing your values to life (Section 1.2). Staying true to your values is a major step towards motivation, enjoyment and fulfilment. Even the pathway to a degree can be part of a fulfilling life! This is about finding resonance in your goals.

How to elevate your motivation

The question to ask here is 'What's important?'. And then, to peel away the layers, keep asking it over and over again until you get to the heart of what matters to you. Eventually you'll find out what your goal really means to you. Knowing this and reminding yourself of why your goal is important helps to build your motivation and keep it strong.

Take a goal that you want to feel more motivated about. Ask 'What's important to me about (achieving) that goal?' And for each answer you give, ask again, 'What's important to me about that?' When you run out of answers you're probably close to knowing what's really important to you about this goal. Notice now what happens to your motivation when you think about what's really important to you.

This is straightforward in principle. In practice it can be hard to get beyond the obvious first few answers. Be patient, try it for a while, maybe come back to it over several days or ask a friend to help by asking you 'What's important?' over and over again.

Tip: you could imagine answers appearing at different levels, for example pretend you're in an elevator and as you go up to each floor you give another answer. Or you could use some steps or stairs offering the next answer as you climb up each one.

2.3   Where are you setting your sights?

Thinking about your goals you can no doubt imagine some fairly predictable things that you'll aim to accomplish that are easily within your reach. You'll pass your essays and exams, keep reasonably healthy, be involved in the odd club or society, and more. What, though, could you probably achieve if you aimed a little higher? Could you pass those exams with a

Only you know where to aim

higher mark, become fitter, take a more active role in a club or society? And, if you fully put your mind to it, what are you really capable of? What, if you were at your very best, might be possible if you set your sights to aim higher still? And what would be a fantasy, a pipe dream, so ridiculous that it makes you laugh to even think of it?

These questions may not be easy to answer. They point to the question of 'Where are you setting your sights?' and how that might affect your motivation. When we ask these questions in workshops students assume we are trying to push them to go further with their goals. In fact this isn't the case. What these questions do is 'test out' where the right place is for you. What motivates you is what motivates you. Some students

want to aim high and challenge themselves with more difficult coursework, taking on lots of things to do and working to tight deadlines. Others want something less taxing and to aim well within what they know they can achieve. So we're not suggesting how challenging your goals should be. We're suggesting that you learn what level of challenge works for you and then set your goals in a way to reflect that. The question is: what gives you motivation and enjoyment, but without boredom or unhelpful anxiety? This is about setting the level of aspiration that excites you.

How to work out where to set your sights

Sometimes you may aim for goals well within your comfort zone and never really find out what you're capable of. At other times you may aim too high, beyond what feels reachable (perhaps based on expectations of others). Either way is a recipe for losing motivation. Here is a way to explore your aspirations and feel the difference between predictable, probable, possible and pipe-dream.

Imagine a continuum set out like this:

Predictable ⟶ Probable ⟶ Possible ⟶ Pipe dream

Take one of your goal areas. The first question to ask is: With little or no challenge what level of achievement is predictable? What's likely to be achieved even if I'm not really trying or I'm distracted? What does this predictable goal look like? How does this feel?

Next ask: With a bit more challenge and application, what level of achievement is probable? If you set your sights to aim for this level what does your more probable goal look like? How do you feel when you think about this?

Now ask: What's possible? If you aim higher, challenge yourself further and tap into your full potential? What could you aspire to? What does your possible goal look like? How does this feel?

Then, with no limits: What's a pipe dream, a fantasy? In a child like world where there are no constraints, where everything and anything is possible... what does your pipe dream goal look like? How does this feel?

Finally, compare what it feels like to aim for each of the four goals. What's the right amount of challenge for you? Where do you want to set your sights? And now, what SMART goal does that mean you'll set? Note that this might be somewhere in between the four points.

Note: these different areas – the predictable, probable, possible and pipe-dream – are not 'steps'. One does not lead to another. For example, you don't have to get a third-class degree result before you get a first-class degree result! They're about where you set your aspiration.

We're not suggesting where you should set your sights, that's down to you. We sometimes find that students stay at the predictable. Sometimes that's right, especially if there are a lot of other things going on in your life that are demanding. However, do check if there are any Gremlins lurking saying 'can't'. Sometimes the 'probable' feels OK. Sometimes the right place is between the probable and the possible, and sometimes it's between the possible and the pipe dream. And sometimes, in reviewing the possibilities, students realise the pipe dream isn't such a pipe dream after all ... the pipe dream becomes what's possible. Only you know what's right for you. The question is, what feels aspiring? What unleashes your passion?

A key point is to experience what it 'feels' like to set your sights at different levels. That means getting out of your 'head space' and into one that's more physical. You can create the continuum on the floor, and place a different coloured card at each of the points along it, writing or drawing the answers to the predictable, probable, possible and pipe dream questions on each card. You can then move along the line to get into the feel of each level and in touch with what's right for you.

Tip: different ways of doing this exercise can make a difference for you. Sticking with the physical you could try using objects to create the continuum – pebbles, stones, fruit – with one dropped at the feet with little or no application (predictable), one dropped at arm's length with a little more application (probable), one placed by lying down and using a stick to push it further away (possible), and one thrown far into the distance (pipe dream). A visual way of doing this could be by imagining you're a garden designer. Pretend you have a blank canvas, bare earth, to work with. Imagine what a predictable design would look like, then, stretching your comfort zone and being progressively more adventurous, picture the probable, possible and pipe dream. What do you see at each level of design?

2.4 Turning goals into action – how much to stretch what you do

It's one thing to have a goal – however aspirational it may be – it's quite another to turn it into action. Sometimes you might be willing to be bold in what you do and take steps that really stretch you. Perhaps you choose an essay that is more challenging and yet will engage and stretch you more. Maybe you dare to put yourself forwards and become the treasurer of your society. Or you take a risk and make a full Sunday Roast for your flat-mates **Find the right stretch for you** or family. And sometimes, even with the aspiration to go for more, you choose to hold back, making more timid moves. You stick with the easiest essay even though it will be hard to make it stand out. You stay as a member of the society helping out without a clear role. Or you make everyone beans on toast for fear of mistiming the oven! Somewhere between being timid and being bold is a pathway of steps towards your goals where what you do, the action you take, is daring enough to feel worthwhile and thrilling. It gives you the right amount of stretch.

Turning goals into action

Some actions just feel too daring, a stretch too far, so you retreat well into your comfort zone to play safe and do something altogether less risky. Between these extremes the in-between can get lost. Here is a way to test in your imagination what it feels like to move between playing safe and being bold in your actions. In doing so you can find out how daring you want to be in order to give you the motivation and thrill to make the most of your goals.

Choose a goal to work with. Now imagine a pathway with seven lines across it. At each line identify an action that you could take that could move you forwards towards your goal. At the first line is the safest thing you could do: Action 1. The last line is the most daring thing you could do: Action 7. This will feel way out of your comfort zone. Now, fill in the gaps at lines 2, 3, 4, 5 and 6 by identifying actions that become progressively more daring and stretching. At each line ask: What's an action that's even more daring than the one before? Once you have got seven possible actions worked out, choose which action you will commit to and when you'll do it.

Motivation is a feeling, so doing this exercise physically may add to your experience. You could use real steps, trees, lampposts, pieces of paper on the floor. With the seven steps mapped out you can move along them to find your desired degree of stretch. Where feels the right balance between playing safe and being bold?

Tip: to get the feel of this in another way, try taking a moment to do some stretching. With your arms by your sides gently lean over to one side, go as far as you comfortably can. Notice that if you leant further it could be a little painful and if you come up a little, you don't feel any stretch. Now, if you wanted to get more flexible, the challenge would be to find that place between comfort and extra stretch. Everyone's stretch is different. How far you stretch is not about how far over you're leaning compared to other people, it's about the right stretch for you.

Not really with it? Getting things done by being focused

How often do you find yourself all over the place? Today's the day you've decided, yet again, to really get down to it. This time you'll really focus. You've set the time aside to start that essay, get that reading done, or go to the gym. Then, before you can say 'focus', the distractions come flooding in. You know what you need to do, you're all set up to do it, and, it just isn't happening. Your mind has wandered elsewhere.

Your attention is distracted by the need to check Facebook. Your friends are offering you more enticing things to do or asking for your help. There are other more pleasant things on offer – computer games, movies, TV, relaxing, coffee, or food. You're worrying about money, other work that needs doing or things at home. You're irritated by the noise upstairs. Urgent things need addressing, like the washing up or that phone call. You start daydreaming about all the possibilities of what you could be doing at the weekend or about your career. Before long you convince yourself it would be better to get started later or the next day. Emotions are calling for your attention. You're worried you might get things wrong, anxious about making a mistake. Then, ironically, to make it worse, you get annoyed at yourself for not being focused, and frustration, guilt, fear or anger can set in.

- What's it like when your day is full of excuses?
- What will it mean when you're doing what's really important?
- What do you gain by putting things off?

When you think about it, it's a wonder you ever find the ability to focus at all! And yet, and in spite of everything, there are times when you can find focus. This chapter is about how you do that and finding ways to do it when you want to. It's about how to manage your distractions and give all your attention to what it is you intend to be doing – in short, to get things done.

FOCUS = BEING PRESENT – DISTRACTION

In this chapter you'll be able to give yourself permission to:

- Look ahead to backwards plan
- Put importance first
- Manage your interferences
- Procrastinate no more!

Students say being distracted is like ...

... Blurred vision ... always looking for the next thing ... living in a dream world ... the world is spinning fast around you ... being pulled in different directions ... 'monkey mind' ... a fidgety child ... things coming at you in all directions ... being bored ... in a busy market place

Students have described being focused like...

... An eagle watching its prey ... a footballer with their eye on the ball ... 'on it like a car bonnet' ... catching a wave ... 'just do it' ... rolling your sleeves up ... keeping the rhythm in a band ... in the zone ... in a bubble ...a tiger

What's it like for you when you're distracted?
What's it like when you're being focused?

Being distracted – whether it's by Facebook, coffee, holidays, self-doubt, friends, home life, noise, your emotions, the news, or whatever else – is a way of being. This takes us right back to the start of this book and the possibility that you can create shifts in perspective that can bring about a different way of being. Other chapters in this book may also be worth exploring to help with being focused:

- Are you distracted by a lack of clarity as to why you're doing a degree? If that's the case you may need to remind yourself what it is about being focused that you value. (See Sections 1.1 and 1.2).
- Is your distraction to do with being out of balance, feeling like things have got out of control and become overwhelming? If this feels the case then it's worth reviewing (Section 7.5).
- Do you find yourself unsure as to what exactly the aim is at this point, what your goals are, what you need to achieve? Are you unsure of whether you're making any progress? If so then working out what your goals are will be a good start.
- Your distractions may be so strong at this point that you need to feel more resilience, to feel in a good place to approach the demands of the degree. You may be experiencing a sense of 'burnout' and exhaustion. As well as building on all of Part I, exploring your resilience could be important here.
- Sometimes your distractions may be from things you can't change and there is a need to accept what is. The mindfulness and meditation exercises in the final chapter could be helpful.

 Finally, are you distracted by a Gremlin? It could be very well disguised, telling you about all the other important things that need doing first. Or it might be very explicit: 'What's the point? It's not going to work'. It could be saying all sorts of things. If Gremlins are your distraction, then employ some Gremlin-busting tricks (see Section 1.3)!

If you've reviewed the questions above and addressed any issues relevant to you, then at this point you'll be clear about needing to find some practical ways to re-find your focus, and that is the focus of the rest of this chapter.

3.1 Looking ahead to backwards plan

When students describe all the things they need to fit in, work, study, societies they're involved in, keeping up with friends, it's no wonder it can be hard to find focus when they need it. There's so much on offer, there's so many opportunities, such a lot to do, new and ongoing responsibilities. All the clubs, societies, friendships, sports, social events, home pressures, work experience. Not to mention your degree, the lectures, seminars, reading to be done, essays to hand in, portfolios to work on, dissertations to complete and more. It can seem like it's all

Everything has its place when you start at the finish

happening at once and as if everything needs doing at the same time. Things mount up, pressure builds, several essays or other pieces of work need to be handed in during the same week, plus there are presentations to work on and exams to revise for. With so much to do and so little time to do it you can find yourself jumping from one thing to another, trying to keep all the plates spinning until ... it all becomes a blur and can be hard to cope with. If you start adding up what you need to do, you start to wish you hadn't – writing yet another 'to do list' only makes it seem worse!

When the pressure mounts and you feel it's impossible to know what to focus on, it can be worth taking a leap forwards to where it is you want to get to, i.e. the completed task or goal, in order to be able to look back and work out what needs to happen and by when. In other words, making a plan! That may sound dull. The beauty of making a plan is being able to play with what needs to happen by when and see things spread out over time rather than all bunched up together. A plan gives everything its time and place, shows what can be left for a while and how it all fits together setting you free to enjoy what you need to focus on now.

How to fit things together over time

The principle is to step forwards to your end point, your goal once achieved, and then look back from the point of completion to see what you did to get there, i.e. what needs to be done by when, also taking into account how long each task will take and how much time to allocate to it. This provides you with a critical path for what needs doing by when. By doing this with all the different things you're juggling, for example working on different essays at the same time, or revising while also going to band practice or Skyping home, you can start to see how you can focus on particular things while everything is moving along in parallel.

Working with a plan in this way can reduce the anxieties that come from muddling through and help you be clearer about whether you're on the right path or not.

Take one of your current projects and try the following:

Step 1. Working backwards from the endpoint, make a list of all the tasks that needed to be done to get there.

Step 2. Order the tasks in terms of what needs to be done first, second, third and so on.

Step 3. For each task, identify how much time is needed, noting some will be larger or smaller than others.

Step 4. Produce a Gantt chart as your plan.

Step 5. Check you've included time in the Gantt chart for things going wrong, taking longer than expected and so on – perhaps an additional 20 per cent of time for each task? This creates a buffer zone that can help to manage the sense of pressure if it feels too much.

Note: you can do a Gantt chart with different timescales allowing different degrees of detail. For example you could do one for the whole year, or for the month ahead, or for a specific project or multiple projects. You can have several Gantt charts working in parallel to help plan when you've different things going on at once.

Tip: if this method feels dull you could imagine approaching this way of planning your work and life in a different way, for example like loading a cargo ship. Your tasks are your cargo and you can play around with different combinations to get all the cargo on board and make sure each piece is loaded in the right order to be able to offload it when you need to.

The Gantt chart (pages 54–55) shows a way of mapping out the different activities you might be involved in, deadlines you need to meet and how they fit together. You can see here there are essays to do that have a similar deadline, for example. You can also see that some activities need particular periods of focus. Some activities may be ongoing (e.g. dotted line) though not a priority at that time. Sometimes the focus of activities overlap with others and sometimes they don't. This is illustrative and in making a Gantt chart you can decide how much detail is useful for you.

Student experience – Charlie

There are times when you have different priorities for things, all of which you want to do well. Charlie, a final year student, found focusing on different important areas a challenge.

"I knew the championships were coming up, and also knew that I had deadlines for university work during the fortnight preceding the contest, and tests scheduled for just after the contest that needed to be done for me to gain a place on a teacher training course following university ... I was spending a lot of time thinking about all the things that needed doing, thinking about how busy I was, but didn't actually start to progress with any of the goals. I sat down over a good coffee with one of my housemates (as all good students do!) and wrote down everything I needed to do on Post-It notes, along with the date they needed to be completed. These then became the cargo, and needed to be fitted into a ship, I drew out a timetable for my week, and started to put things into the timetable that needed to be done. When I could see smaller time pockets emerging during my week, I could drop in activities such as practising my violin, in small chunks that fitted around other commitments. I continued until I had a two-week period planned out that contained everything that needed to be done. I could see that there was also 'down time' included. I've learnt when I try and plan my time, I spend an awful lot of time thinking about what needs to be done, and not actually getting cracking with things. I also tend to over-dramatise what needs to be done, making out that I have so much to do, and get carried away complaining about that, rather than actually looking what I can fit in where. After doing this task, I have also found that I tend to over-estimate the time it takes to do things, and tend to think I couldn't practise my violin for anything less than 45 minutes at a time, whereas in reality, a period of 15–30 minutes is much more realistic, and more manageable. I managed to get through the two weeks leading up to the music contest, and after spending long periods of time beforehand complaining that I wouldn't get through it alive, I am definitely still here, and even enjoying things like being able to find time to practise my violin in amongst everyday things like lectures!"

Gantt Chart

	Tasks	Week 1	Week 2	Week 3	Week 4
Essay 1	Read around				
	Choose topic	→→→		★	
	Reading			———	
	First draft				
	Comments from friend				
	Additional reading				
	Final draft				
	Hand in				
Essay 2	Read around		→→→		
	Choose topic				★
	Reading		- - - - - - - - - - -		
	First draft				
	Comments from friend				
	Additional reading				
	Final draft				
	Hand in				
Group project	Meetings		★		★
	Collect and analyse data			→→→	
	Prepare PowerPoint				
	Presentation				
Exam	Revision				
Theatre production	Design props	→→→→			
	Make model props			→→→→	
	Final props				
Weekend away					

Week 5	Week 6	Week 7	Week 8	Week 9	Week 10

3.2   Putting importance first

Jeff recalls how a student once said at a workshop, 'I've just made a note on my 'to do list' to write another 'to do' list!' This student was not alone. More time can be spent on writing lists than doing what's on them. When there's so much to be done, so many tasks to juggle, the habit of writing lists, Post-It note reminders, or inputting tasks onto your phone can become addictive. Once you have a 'to do list', it's funny how 'urgent' some things can become. In fact so much time can be spent clearing the seemingly urgent tasks off your list that by the time you get to some of the really core things that need doing yet which

> **Having a to do list is not the same as prioritising your day**

don't feel so urgent, either more 'to dos' have appeared or you've lost the concentration, energy or even motivation to focus on what's really important. The trouble is urgent things feel pressing regardless of how important they are and consequently often take precedence over other more important matters. You find yourself always responding to urgent things because, over time, the important things have been put off or delayed and have now also become urgent. A great recipe for overload and never feeling like you are on top of things.

Creating lists to help you remember your 'to dos' is not the same as planning how to prioritise your day. The way you balance urgency and importance when you work out how to juggle your tasks can mean the difference between feeling really focused and feeling really distracted. The question is then, how can you organise yourself in a way that means you give yourself permission to get on with the important things without being a slave to things that appear to become urgent? This is a really important distinction. Urgent things, because they are urgent, can feel important. Will remembers a secretary at work who had a sign on his desk that read: 'Don't make your bad planning my urgent work'. The trick here is in learning to prioritise in such a way that you get to work on the important things before they become urgent while also dealing with the urgent tasks that come up in a way that stops them becoming too important! For example, leaving it until the last minute to talk to a tutor, and then realising they are off ill! Suddenly what is important becomes urgent and … not possible. Making a distinction between urgent and important is useful both in planning ahead, as well as for reassessing priorities in crisis moments.

 How to put the important things first – a question of priority

When it comes to working from a 'to do list' students often feel that the 'urgent' thing is the most important and must be done first. Then, over time, the important things that didn't get done mount up to become really 'urgent' and that is when pressure and distraction can build. By choosing to make importance be a key principle to guide your prioritisation, you'll find you've more energy and focus for getting the important things done, while 'urgent' things, when really urgent, can still get done.

Step 1. Identify all the things you want to get done today.

Step 2. Order these tasks in terms of importance. Think about your vision, values and goals to help do this.

Step 3. Rank these tasks in terms of urgency. Think about deadlines and be clear about the difference between things that feel urgent or pressing, often other people's urgency, and things that really do need doing now.

Step 4. Identify the time each task will take.

Step 5. Plan your day to get the right balance of importance and urgency for you. You can, if you like, think of this as your prioritised 'to do list'.

Note: explore the best time for planning. Is it the day before, to help you switch off? Or is it first thing in the morning, to help you get the feel for the day? Some people like to tick off what they have done at the end of the day to get a feeling of progress.

Tip: if you want to be playful in working out your priorities, you could imagine you're a juggler and each ball represents a task. You can pick up each 'task' to weigh up the feeling of urgency and importance. If you were to juggle the balls, which would you start with? How many in total? If you juggle them all, which would you least want to drop and which would you choose to drop first to make juggling more do-able?

Student experience – James

There are times when there is a lot to juggle to get your university work done, let alone other things you have to organise. James was struggling to fit in all his coursework while preparing for a fieldtrip abroad:

"I was experiencing the feeling that I needed to get a lot done, and wasn't able to get everything done within the short time frame of a week. Having attempted to juggle some tennis balls, I realised that the only task with a time pressure was the poster for coursework that needed handing in on the Friday. This was the first task that I saw needed to be completed, because it was a group effort, but also I saw that because it was a group activity, there wasn't as much weight behind it than if it was an individual piece of coursework. The least important ball to pick up was the finishing of lecture notes, which I realised, could be completed after I return from the field course. By going through the motions of physically thinking about each task individually, I was able to think about the importance, and feel the weight of each task in my hand, as I held and attempted to juggle the balls. Through doing this activity, I was able to realise that during the week, I only actually had to complete the poster, and then could spend more time packing and preparing for the field course. I have left the completing of lecture notes for when I return from the field course, and have noticed that I will have a large period of time travelling to the airport and then on the plane in which I could do some reading and note taking for the field course, meaning that I don't have to dedicate too much time beforehand, which could be better spent doing other tasks.

I am not sure what's going to happen after the field course, and how this activity will impact on me in the future, because I am leaving to go on the field course tomorrow, so I guess only time will tell …"

3.3 Managing your interferences

Even the best-laid plans can get disrupted. You don't find a space in the library. The coach gets delayed coming back from the away game. Your laptop crashes. A friend has a disaster and needs help. You misjudged your bank account. You dropped the spaghetti on the floor. Things can go wrong or may not work out as intended, the unexpected happens. They seem unavoidable. At the same time, there are those things that you let get in the way. Perhaps an offer of coffee with a friend, a TV programme you can't resist, a Skype back home, a Facebook message or some pleasant daydreaming about the weekend. It might be these things need your attention, and if that's the case, it's your choice to devote time to them. The question is, how aware are you of your interferences? And then, how often do you get distracted by interferences you could avoid?

Stop distractions by being more honest

How to be in control of your interferences

By being more aware, and indeed, more honest, about interferences, you can identify which ones you can manage, and which ones you can't. Sometimes spotting them is enough. Equally, working out what you can and can't control is particularly useful when followed by deciding to take action on what you can.

Step 1. Over a period of a few days, make a note of interferences that distract you.

Step 2. Which on your list of interferences are down to you, and which are down to others or something else? To put it another way, which do you 'self-generate' and which happen because of other people or things?

Step 3. What could you do to better manage the self-generated interferences? For example, planning times to look at Facebook or make overseas Skype calls, or arranging when to meet a friend rather than leaving it unplanned. How many of your interferences come from not dealing with the important things in a timely way, i.e. putting first things first (see Section 3.2).

Step 4. Looking at your list of interferences down to other people or other things, what could you do to better manage those? For example how do you allow other people to interrupt you? What actions could you take or boundaries could you put in place to stop that? How could you plan for other things that go wrong? Do you need to have other 'back-up' plans in place?

Note that there may be some more searching questions for you to think on:

• What are you attributing more importance to when you allow other people's agendas to take over your own?

• When people interrupt you, how honest are you being with yourself and with them?

• What kind of boundaries do you set to protect your time, energy and space? Do you let others trespass too easily? What conversations might you need to have to re-establish the boundaries?

• When do the results of putting things off come back to cause interference now?

Tip: you need to tune in your radar and be honest to spot interferences. You could imagine you have a CCTV camera watching you, so that nothing gets missed. Or perhaps you're being watched by a referee who gives out yellow and red cards every time they spot an interference. Exchanging a list with a friend might provoke you both to see things you'd not admitted to seeing.

Examples of interferences students have identified:

IT problems	Other students
Fancying someone	Tutors
Daydreams	Coffee
Interruptions	Non-productive meetings
Going off at tangents	Money
Noise	Late night out
Being late	Being early
Forgetting things	Not making decisions
Procrastination	Text messages
Lacking motivation	Gremlins
Facebook	Emails
Too much to do	Friends
Accommodation worries	Family troubles
Career activities	

3.4 Procrastinate no more!

Why not leave it until tomorrow? When you really don't feel like doing something, how much better it feels to put it off for a while. That bit of

reading, making a start on your assignment, phoning an old friend, going for a swim, pulling your CV together, job searches. There are, of course, all sorts of excuses on hand to put things off. It's too late to start it now. You're not in the mood. One more day won't make a difference. I need more time to plan. I'll just do a little job first. I need to be doing something else. I'd rather be doing something else. There was no one to ask. I felt a bit poorly. I'm hung-over. No doubt you can add to these. Whether it's for your degree studies, towards your life plans or even for your enjoyment now, you may find yourself putting all sorts of things off. Indeed, ironically, you may find you put things off that once you do get started you really enjoy

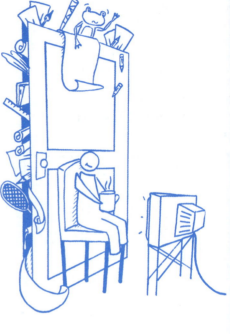

– think about phoning old friends, playing a sport, a musical instrument, writing a poem, baking a cake.

There are lots of reasons we put things off. To address some of those you may need to explore other chapters. As a minimum, if you have them, make sure you've got your self-doubting Gremlins in check (Section 1.3). Also be clear on why you value the task at hand (Section 1.2), have a sense of balance in mind (Section 7.5), and be clear about what your goals are. You also need to have given yourself permission to focus, to have established putting the important things first, and started to manage interferences. If there is an underlying fear that means you put things off, you may find it helpful to explore the visualisation in the final chapter (Section 8.4).

Giving up putting off!

The principle involves working out what you gain and what you lose from putting something off, and noticing what's stopping you from getting started. Though you might really want to get something done, there's something that is stopping you. While that can involve all sorts of interferences explored in other sections, there might be other reasons underlying your procrastination. Recognising what's really stopping you is an important step.

Think of something important that you've been putting off then consider the following:

Step 1. Being really honest, what's stopping you from making a start? Is this about a fear of some kind? Is it to do with your confidence in being able to complete it? Is it a lack of skill or knowledge? Is the enormity of the task too great to make a start feel worthwhile or even possible? Do you lack the creativity, the energy, the courage?

Step 2. What's the cost of putting it off? What do you gain by putting it off? How much energy are you expending avoiding this? What excuses are you making? What will happen in the long run if you keep putting this off? What does putting it off say about you?

Step 3. What will you gain by getting this done? What will make it feel worthwhile? What rewards could you give yourself along the way? How much energy or peace of mind will you get from moving forwards? How will you feel once it's done?

Step 4. What needs to happen to get on with this? What small steps can you take to make a start? What's one small thing you could do first? What will make it easier/ more fun to get started? What space do you need to create? Who could you be accountable to?

Tip: sometimes it's hard to get the distance from something to ask these questions. A variation on the above that can help is to use an object to represent the thing you're putting off – choose something that resonates with you in some way. Put the object in front of you and while focusing on it ask yourself the questions in Step 1. Then try picking up the object in one hand and ask the questions in Step 2. Then pick it up in the other hand and ask the questions in Step 3. Placing it down again, ask the questions in Step 4. What's changed when you look at it now, and in how you think about what you've been putting off?

Note: you may find a pattern to your procrastination- a common reason why you find yourself procrastinating. Pay attention to that. What would it mean to address the common issue?

Student experience – Chris

Sometimes it can feel like everything needs to be done at the same time and you can find yourself putting things off. Chris found himself overwhelmed:

"During the run-up to the beginning of second term, I was faced with a plethora of deadlines, each requiring me to complete copious amounts of reading on top of the suggested course reading. Due to this seemingly unfathomable sum of work I began to panic and stress when I even thought about doing the work and procrastinated as a means of coping. These feelings were made evermore copious due to my wanting to complete this work well in advance of the deadlines presented. I decided to remove myself from the situation at hand by going on a long walk and organise my thoughts. This was achieved through rationalising my current situation and weighing up my desired completion dates in relation to the actual deadlines and considering how much work I had already completed. Through such a process I realised that the pressure I was feeling was not coming from the work but from myself, setting high targets in terms of workload that were unrealistic and, resultantly, incapacitating my ability to work effectively through this stress. Following this realisation I have amended my work planning to be more realistic in terms of workload and given a greater consideration to the timeframe this can be achieved in. This has also enabled me to plan time within which I can relax and pursue hobbies. Through this exercise I was able to calm myself and proceed with the work I had to do, applying myself with more focus and improving my time management."

Lost your confidence? Finding it as a question of emphasis

Sometimes losing your confidence can come from nowhere and really knock you sideways. Despite all you've achieved to get to university, it's still so easy to lose your confidence, with the knock on effect this can have on your study, social life or university experience as a whole. Universities are full of people who know a lot more than you or can do things better than you. Other students appear so popular and at ease with everybody. There are students with incredible skills and talents in sport, music, politics, language etc. They can even make the perfect Sunday roast! Perhaps you were used to being top of the class at school, or the captain of your sports team, only to discover at university a whole bunch of other people who were top of their class or captains of their teams.

It follows that, if finding your confidence is going to depend on how well other people are doing or by what you think others think of you, you're in for a bumpy ride. Other people can of course be a great source of inspiration. A competitive moment can be a boost to motivation. Good feedback on your essays can be really affirming. However, your confidence is going to be pretty fragile if it depends on external factors like these.

CONFIDENCE = SELF-BELIEF – SELF-DOUBT

The good news is this: confidence need not depend on how good you are at something or on what others say. Think of two students, both doing equally well in their studies. One will feel confident, taking everything in their stride, seeming to find it all straightforward and having a good balance between work and play. The other is constantly worried, anxious that they've not done enough, always studying, and when they're not studying, worrying about what they should be studying. Indeed, sometimes there are students who exude confidence even though they're quite average in their results.

- What will you gain as your confidence grows?
- How do you undermine your self-belief?
- What will being more confident say about you?

Finding confidence, then, isn't about anything 'out there'. Instead, confidence is about what's within you and what you choose to emphasise. That is, whether you choose to focus on feeding self-doubt, or whether you choose to emphasise your self-belief.

This chapter looks at how to find your confidence within by:

- Tapping into your confidence when you need it
- Making confidence a habit
- Being clear on who you are doing things for
- Playing to your strengths

Students say when they've lost their confidence it feels like ....
    ... my knees are made of jelly ... all empty inside ... I daren't look at anyone ... hunched up in a tiny ball ... a weight on my shoulders ... everything goes black ... I can't move

And have described being confident as like ...
    ... eating my favourite ice cream ... wearing a bullet proof vest ... the sun is shining ... being the Incredible Hulk ...having a force field around me ... feeling ten-foot tall ... smiling ...

The following section will help you find your confidence now. Themes in other chapters will also contribute to building your confidence. For example, getting things done, getting a better balance (Section 7.5) and building your resilience will all contribute to your confidence. Building confidence takes practice, though. You can't become a confident long-distance runner immediately, yet you can feel confident of your running abilities right now and build from there. So, being confident is about knowing what you're capable of now, and knowing that you can be capable of more in the future. It's knowing that your confidence lies within you.

4.1 Tapping into your confidence when you need it

We said in the introduction to this chapter that confidence is about self-belief, not how good you are at something. That means confidence is more to do with how you're being than the result of what you're doing. Given that, to find your confidence you need to pay attention to how you're being. This implies that confidence doesn't need to depend on whether something goes well or not. Instead, even if something doesn't work out as you hoped, you can still feel confident and believe in yourself. Whatever happens, you can handle it!

Real confidence comes from within, whatever happens

One way to think about this is to imagine being confident, even if you're not! Indeed, you can even play a trick to test this out by deciding that, in whatever situation you find yourself, you can act as if you're confident. It's a switch to finding a place of confidence within, an inner belief in your abilities, a confidence based on self-belief, a confidence to be able to handle whatever comes your way. That's the focus here: how to feel confident, despite and with everything around you!

 Your Gremlins may be quite loud in an attempt to stop you exploring your confidence. We suggest that to keep them quiet you do whatever it is that you've found works (see Section 1.3).

How to tap into your confidence

Confidence is a feeling and you can create that feeling with your imagination. By recalling a past event when you felt confident, you can experience a confident feeling in the present moment. The more vividly you recall the memory and bring it alive with the associated sounds, smells, images and sensations then the stronger the feeling. While doing this, you can use a 'trigger' to remind you of this experience in the future, a technique called 'anchoring'. Athletes often use an anchor at the start of an event to get into their 'zone', as do actors, musicians and public speakers. With practice you can use your anchor – a gesture, a word, an image – to tap into feeling confident, whatever the situation.

Step 1. Choose your anchor: a physical gesture and a word that you can use to trigger being confident. For example gestures like clenching your fist, squeezing thumb and middle finger together, rubbing an ear lobe. Words like 'Yes' or 'Wow' or 'I can'. Choose what's right for you.

Step 2. Think of a time when you felt really confident. It doesn't matter how long ago this was, so long as you can remember it. Perhaps it was during school days, maybe doing a sport, playing music, other hobby, socialising with friends. What's important isn't what happened before, or after, rather the very moment when you felt confident.

Step 3. Remember that moment vividly and bring it alive. What were you doing? Who was around you? What were you wearing? What could you see? What could you hear? How did you feel? What sensations were you feeling in your body? What could you smell?

Step 4. Stay in the moment. Try making the images brighter, more colourful and bigger; the sounds louder and crisper. What intensifies the feeling of confidence for you? Find out what works and make the feeling as strong as you can. Notice your posture, your head, shoulders, back and your breathing. This is your physiology when you're being confident.

Step 5. Keeping your feeling and physiology of confidence, let an image come to mind that connects to being confident.

Step 6. Now set your anchor. Keeping your feeling of confidence strong make the gesture you chose at the start and say the word. Hold the gesture for at least ten seconds and repeat the word over and over if you want to.

If you need to, repeat any of the steps above. To make the anchors work even better, you can practise them over time. Several times a day for two weeks works well.

When will tapping into your confidence be useful to you?

Students have pointed to using anchoring when:

- They have been in seminars and not felt confident to ask questions
- Writing an essay under pressure in an exam when feeling insecure
- Presenting a project and being worried they'll look a fool
- Playing a sport and holding back for fear of making a mistake
- They've been told they will never be able to do something
- Entering a room full of people they don't know
- Putting themselves forward for a role organising a student society

In all these contexts – and more – ask, 'What difference would it make if I felt more confident?'

Student experience – Danny

Sometimes you can use confidence from one situation and bring it to another. Danny was worried about giving a presentation:

"Last year I was required to give a presentation on my dissertation topic to a group of 20 of my peers. Public speaking is not my forté and, as it got closer to my turn to present, I began to feel more and more nervous. My pulse elevated and worry began gnawing away at what little confidence I had to begin with. To combat this (so I could actually function!) I thought back to a time when I've been very confident and, for this particular time, chose an anchor at a point when I felt confident in front of a large audience. Thus, I chose a time when I played in a band in front of 300 people. I thought back to how it felt and what made me feel that way. I knew exactly what I was doing and I was enjoying what I was doing. After these thoughts, I realised that what I was about to do was not so different – I'd thought a lot about my topic, practised the presentation with friends and enjoyed the topic I was presenting on. This made me feel much more confident with what I was about to do and, if I could feel that confident in front of 300 people, then why not 20 of my peers? Using my confidence anchor and putting the current task into perspective allowed me to give an effective presentation."

4.2   Making confidence a habit

When you think about your day, it's quite surprising to realise just how much you do things on autopilot, without really thinking about it. Indeed, you do much of what you do through habit and routine, and you might say that's a good thing too. Having to consciously assess every situation and make an active decision as to what to do could become quite tedious. At the same time, you probably also have bad habits. Those things that are so automatic you don't really think about them and find hard to stop. When it comes to confidence the same is true. There are some habits that will support your confidence, and some that undermine.

> **Enough things can knock your confidence without you adding to them**

One question then is, do you have habits that undermine your confidence, whether in your studies, social life, creativity, sports, thinking about careers, etc? And, following a proposition made by Aristotle of all people, that excellence itself is a habit , can you start to find habits, things you do repeatedly, that can fuel your self-belief and build your confidence?

 ### How to make confidence a habit

Working out which habits make you feel confident and emphasising these is one way to keep your confidence topped up. Equally important is noticing which habits fuel self-doubt and drain confidence. In other words, doing more of the things that make you feel good about yourself and less of the things that don't can reinforce your feeling of confidence. Changing habits isn't always easy, and so here we provide a structure to help.

Begin by creating a list of the habits that make you feel confident and good about yourself. These are habits that fuel your confidence – we'll call them 'uppers'. Create a second list of the habits that don't make you feel confident – these are the 'downers' that drain your confidence.

Habits come in all shapes and forms and often go unnoticed so here are some tips for things you might look out for, habits of:

- Thoughts or day dreams
- Debriefing after meetings or at the end of the day
- Eating and drinking
- Conversations
- What you prioritise
- How you start your day
- Who you spend time with
- When you take breaks
- What you do with breaks

- Planning the day
- Setting goals
- What you get done
- What you put off
- What you wear
- Personal care
- How you relax
- What you say to yourself

Some habits may have become rigid self-imposed rules which you feel you mustn't break. They may be re-enforced by the words of your oh-so-lovely Gremlin friends – 'should', 'shouldn't', 'must', 'have to', 'ought not' … For example, 'Must always go along with what others think', or 'Should always do what I'm told', or 'Ought to go out on Friday night with flatmates'.

Now, considering your habits, the uppers and the downers, what do you want to change? If it helps, instead of lists, try a mind map or use pictures or objects to represent habits, do what works for you.

To change a habit you may find two things useful. Firstly set a clear goal to change. For example pick one particularly draining 'downer' that you're going to do less of or stop altogether, and pick one 'upper' that you want to emphasise more. Being more precise can make the intention feel more real – how much less, how much more? Chapter 2 on goal setting may be worth re-visiting to make sure your goal motivates you.

Secondly you can create a new structure to help change your habits. By this we mean putting something in place, a framework, to support the changes you want to make. For example if you've decided you want to start your day earlier then an alarm clock that wakes you at 8.00 am each morning is an example of a structure. A bell that goes off every hour to remind you to drink water is another. If you want to eat less chocolate then having fruit to hand and no chocolate in the cupboard is another. Creating a structure makes changing habits easier.

Examples of habits students have identified

Students have identified all sorts of habits that knock their confidence:

Downers

- Staying in bed longer
- Not reading for seminars
- Turning up late
- Under-preparing for projects
- Talking negatively
- Leaving essays to the last minute
- Spending too much time on social media and texting
- Spending time with certain people
- Reminding themselves of their mistakes
- Not taking care of themselves
- Habitual eating

Students have also identified all sorts of habits that build their confidence:

Uppers

- Aim to ask at least one question in a lecture
- Have a regular routine
- Plan essays early
- Meet friend at the gym
- Dressing well
- Phone a friend every Sunday night
- Not leaving things to the last minute
- Get up the same time each day
- Join clubs
- Read at least one piece of work a day
- Smile at people

4.3   Being clear on who you're doing things for

Following the suggestion we've made that confidence is not to do with how good you are, it would also be fair to say that your confidence is going to be on shaky ground if it's based on what others think of you. If your confidence is based on approval from others you'll often find you're having to second-guess what people are thinking about you. This can lead to a lot of misunderstanding. In university life where there are so many people to gain approval from, it can also be exhausting. In the process of wanting to please those around you – your new friends, your old friends, your lecturers/tutors, your family – you may find you lose confidence in the ability to know what matters to you in deciding what to say yes or no to.

You're faced with a lot of decisions in university life. Decisions about what modules to take, which coursework to do, how to use your time, what to do in the evenings, how to use your money well, what to eat, which friends to see, when to visit home, how to get a job, what career you want, what to do for a dissertation. With some of those decisions it will be absolutely right to keep in mind the approval of others. For example, you might need approval from your dissertation supervisor about your methodology, you may need approval from your sports team about a training regime, approval from your partner about working late, or you could need discussion with your flatmates about the music you want to play. At the same time, it's also important for your confidence that you know what matters to you in those decisions. For example, what dissertation topic will keep you curious and interested, what training regime works in light of your other priorities, whether or not you want to go out with your flat mates? At times, particularly if your confidence is low, you may find it difficult to know whether you're doing something for yourself or for the approval of others.

Sometimes, putting yourself first is just what others need

Worse still, you might even feel selfish in just thinking about what's important to you let alone making a decision based on that. The idea of putting yourself first may feel just not right or confusing. There's a different perspective on this. Would it not be true that when you're at your best, fulfilled and feeling confident in yourself, you're most able to give more to others? Might it be the case that through confidence in what you're doing and why you're doing it, that you can forge much more authentic and sincere relationships? Indeed, doing something to seek 'approval' from others is quite different from doing something for others. People often talk about finding the 'win-win' situation. In this sense you can be doing something for self-fulfilment at the same time as meeting the needs of others. What that means, though, is not meeting the needs of others because you're seeking their approval but because meeting their needs is something you value in itself.

Guilt may play a role here and, while it's often said that this is a wasted emotion that doesn't lead anywhere useful, a guilt-fuelled Gremlin may still pop up and try to get in your way. You 'ought not' or 'must do' … As you try this next exercise, do you want to do it to gain approval from your Gremlin, or for what really matters to you? (See Section 1.3)

How to get clear about who you're doing things for

You can find a balance between meeting your needs for self-fulfilment and seeking the approval of others in what you do and how you are. Sometimes there's a perfect match, other times a tension, and sometimes you may not really know why you've said yes to doing something or being in a particular way. Knowing your intention can be a helpful way to boost your confidence in how you approach a decision or situation. You can test your motives by exploring the extent to which you're doing something for self-fulfilment or for the approval of others and see how this feels.

To do this you can experiment with the following continuum:

Self-fulfilment ◄――――――――► Approval from others

You can try this in relation to your university experience as a whole, or something more specific about your studies, or a particular area of your life. The question to ask is: Who am I doing this for? Where on the line do you find the answer? What does this feel like? How is your level of confidence?

Experience what happens as you move from one end of the continuum to the other. What happens to your confidence if you move towards 'approval from others'? How does it feel to be making decisions based more on being motivated by gaining approval from others than by your own self-fulfilment? What if you move towards the other end of the line, self-fulfilment, how does that feel? In each case, go all the way to the end, take it to the extreme and test it out. What happens to your confidence? After experimenting choose where you would most like to be on the line. Where's the best balance for you? Where's the best place for your confidence? Is this where you were before, or have you moved position?

Tip: we recommend that as well as doing the exercise in your head you try involving physical movement to help really feel the difference. You can do this by using an imaginary line on the floor between two objects then moving along this. Alternatively try placing two objects on the table and a third object (you) in-between.

Examples of balancing tricky decisions

- Wanting the mark but wanting to write an essay for yourself
- Spending time with others when you feel like your own space
- Producing course work that isn't really you
- Pressure to go out when you feel like staying in
- Pressure to dress or behave in a way that doesn't fit your values
- Spending time with people you don't particularly like
- Following a course of action because others think you should
- Sticking with your subject even though you've realised it's not for you
- Staying at university when deep down it's not working for you
- Phoning home each week

Student experience – Emma

When you find yourself needing to make a big decision, it can be good to do so from a place of confidence. Emma found herself reassessing her degree choice at the end of the first year:

"I applied the confidence challenge to my choice of degree modules in the first year of Geography at Lancaster. During the year, I was advised to study both human and physical geography but after studying human geography, I realised that it wasn't what I wanted to do. This resulted in part of my first year being not very enjoyable and I became demotivated and lacked confidence in my abilities. By carrying out the Get Sorted confidence exercise, I imagined the continuum of self-fulfilment as a sunny day at one end, and the other end of the continuum as being a rainy day, representing approval from others. When I placed my topic on the continuum it was closer to the rainy day and further from the sunny day of self-fulfilment. Being at this point on the continuum meant it lowered my confidence and the feeling of demotivation talked about previously was reflected by the cloudy and rainy image in my imagination. As I moved along the continuum towards the self-fulfilment, my confidence level increased. By carrying out the exercise it made me realise that I would rather be nearer to the self-fulfilment end of the continuum. It also made me realise that in life sometimes you have to be in the middle of the continuum with certain situations. Moving on from this exercise, in my next year of university, I am studying subjects that I personally have chosen which will increase my confidence and motivate me to work better."

Student experience – Fenfang

Deciding what you are doing for yourself, and what you are doing for others, can relate really strongly to your values and your self-esteem. Fenfang gives two examples of the challenges involved:

"I want other peoples' approval of my art work. Anxious because I got self fulfilment but not public approval of my creation. I know I am not a professional and that makes me feel inferior or less than other people, such as I do not know how to use Illustrator [a software for digital drawings]. I used to be a person who was proud to stay as who I am and told others not to change yourself because of others' comments. But then lately I have been desperate to get Likes and Followers for my account. I realised I lost sight of being who I am. The continuum of Self-fulfilment—Approval from others is a good exercise to remind me from time to time, both self-fulfilment and approval from others are important for self-esteem. Balance is the most important lesson I learnt here. If I stayed in the past and only think about self-fulfilment, I will not listen to others and will not explore more on what I can do to improve, but I will stay as content and satisfied for my own sake. If I only think about approval from others I would do things that can be totally opposite to the values I hold. Also, my self-esteem will fluctuate because how I feel about myself would completely depend on how other people see me. But I might get approval from the society if I succeed."

"Another example would be how I dress and my attitude on the use of cosmetics. As cosmetics and casual wear were forbidden in my high school, we students did not care much about how we look like without made up (this is our culture, this is stereotyped to be a good student, you don't do made up!) I might even feel odd when there are something 'extra' on my face. But when I got into university, everyone seems to know loads about fashion and make up, that made me uncomfortable. The need to do the same and the desire to stay who I am conflicts strongly. I do admit as an international student, how you dress up affects how the locals react to a great extent. We human beings are visual animals and our first impression of other people greatly depend on their faces and clothes.

So, even though I am staying as who I am deeply inside, I am starting to appreciate fashion and try to experiment a little bit more on the outside, in order to get approval of the local university students. Even though approval from others are not my first priority in life, to change yourself and adapt to new environment are important to all people want to be successful, this little changes of myself are the things I can do, so why not? After all, to change on the outside might not be a bad thing at all, you can always go back to wear the same thing if you do not feel like it, as long as you are staying as a good person and have a good heart, you will win someone's heart.

To conclude, to change yourself on the outside is something extra you can do to win other people's approval, or in some situations a kind of respect. We do need other peoples' approval as a social animal, but keeping the core nice and firm is more important in an ever-changing society."

4.4   Playing to your strengths

Unless you're somehow a very unusual being – and congratulations if you are, though it must feel a bit of a burden – you can't be good at everything. There are some things you're better at than others and some things you just don't take to. The question is, which do you emphasise? People are often quick to think of things they're not good at, their weaknesses, but when it comes to what they're good at they find this

Give your strengths a chance to flourish

hard. Focusing on what you're not good at is a great way to drain your confidence. Indeed, it's a great way to fuel up any self-doubting Gremlins. Like the infamous 'red pen' that shows what's wrong with your coursework, it can be all too easy to overlook your strengths. What might happen to your confidence if you changed focus and asked, 'What am I best at?'

 Gremlins may encourage you not to notice your strengths. How arrogant you must be to dare to think you're good at something! Use your strength now to keep any Gremlins quiet! (See Section 1.3)

How to play to your strengths

It's easy to focus only on weaknesses, a habit that can fuel self-doubt and undermine your confidence. The principle here is to switch emphasis to focus on your strengths. There are a range of situations you can use to help highlight your strengths as well as to acknowledge them on a regular basis. You can also learn to bring your strengths to the forefront more often in what you do and build on them for the future.

Here's a way to do this. In each of the following situations notice your strengths both in what you're doing and how you're being – write them down:

- When you're at your best
- When you feel the most energised
- When you feel the happiest
- When you're doing something particularly well
- When faced with a situation you really didn't like, what strengths did you draw upon to manage?
- What strengths would others see in you? You could ask someone you trust
- When you were really frustrated, because you couldn't make the most of your abilities/potential, what strengths weren't you utilising?

Now you have a list of strengths. You can consolidate this into six key strengths and create a structure to remind you of these each day. Examples of structures include a list you look at, Post-It notes, screensaver, a special object or an image you create. You could also think of other ways to remind you of your strengths – for example, what animal, film star, sports person, or hero would epitomise your strengths?

As a next step, how well do you play to your strengths each day? Are some underused or perhaps lying dormant, kept hidden? You can create a table and score each strength out of ten to represent how well you use it then set a goal to use a particular strength more often. The more specific you can get in terms of context the more helpful this will be. Chapter 2 on goal setting can be worth re-visiting to make sure the goal motivates you. What will you gain by emphasising playing to your strengths more often?

Finally, how does it feel to take time to acknowledge your strengths? Uplifting, awkward, rewarding, strange or a combination of things? What do you notice happening to your feeling of confidence?

Some possible strengths*

Creativity, Originality, Ingenuity, Curiosity, Interest, Novelty-seeking, Openness to experience, Open-mindedness, Judgement, Critical thinking, Love of learning, Perspective, Wisdom, Bravery, Valour, Persistence, Perseverance, Industriousness, Integrity, Authenticity, Honesty, Vitality, Zest, Enthusiasm, Vigour, Energy, Love, Kindness, Generosity, Nurturance, Care, Compassion, Altruistic love, Niceness, Social intelligence, Emotional intelligence, Personal intelligence, Citizenship, Social responsibility, Loyalty, Teamwork, Fairness, Leadership, Forgiveness, Humility, Modesty, Prudence, Self-regulation, Self-control, Appreciation of beauty and excellence, Gratitude, Hope, Optimism, Humour, Playfulness, Spirituality

* The information above is based on the book *Character Strengths and Virtues: A Handbook and Classification* written by Christopher Peterson and Martin Seligman, Published by Oxford University Press and the American Psychological Association (Copyright 2004 by Values in Action Institute) http://www.authentichappiness.sas.upenn.edu/aiesec/content. aspx?id=821

Awaken your creative explorer

How often have you been asked to 'creatively explore' or 'creatively discuss' an idea at university? While some disciplines do so, and indeed, universities are starting to identify 'creative thinking' skills as part of the core skills you might learn, you probably find yourself more often than not being asked to use your critical thinking and evaluation skills. That's great; they have a purpose and we all need to draw on our critical faculties from time to time. There are times, though, when more creative exploration is needed. You might be stuck in your studies, somehow unable to move forwards with a piece of coursework, a project, or with understanding an idea. Some students also feel stuck in other areas – dealing with difficult flatmates, managing home life, responding to cultural differences, wondering how to make more of your spare time, how to get better at your sport, music or art or some other talent, struggling to manage money.

Or maybe you're stuck when you think about the future, life after your degree and beyond? Indeed, you may not be stuck as such, and rather looking for that something extra, for fresh ideas, to enhance, add to, or to develop. When you generate ideas you have options. When you have options you have choice. When you have choice university life feels so much different. There are choices to be made about doing your coursework, approaching reading, what you get from lectures, how to deal with friends, how to spend your spare time, how to manage money, how to manage home life, how to think about your future.

Though it may not feel like it at times, being creative comes naturally to all of us. The problem is, somewhere along the line, we often learn how not to be. Your natural creative explorer will dive back under the duvet at any sign of evaluation, attention to detail and practicalities. Your creativity might also become a little stifled if it all remains in the head, without any

- Where would some new ideas be useful for you?
- What stops you being creative?
- Which values will you be honouring by being more creative?

connection to your other senses, the visceral nature of hunches, gut feelings, intuitions. You can also find your creative explorer rather under-stimulated if it doesn't make contact with others whom it can bounce ideas off.

CREATIVITY = EXPLORATION – EVALUATION

This chapter is about how you can allow your creative explorer to do what it does best: be creative! To stimulate your creative side you'll need to find out, creatively of course, what works for you. We'll offer you some themes, ideas even, that you can experiment with. In this chapter you'll find out how to:

- Turn off the evaluator and let your ideas flow
- Use an Ideas Generator to stimulate fresh possibilities
- Create from more of your senses and intuition
- Create creative conversations

Students say being stuck or having no ideas is like …
    … banging your head against a brick wall … being trapped in a cage … being up a dead end with nowhere to go … feeling anxious … being bored … want escape … stressful … struggling to wake up … an empty landscape

Students say being creative is like …
    … a bolt from the blue … a flash of light … the penny drops … a wide open space … running without getting tired … time flies … time stands still … aha … a flower opening … my tummy tingles … light and fun … having a double espresso…free dance

 As you look at this chapter watch out for any Gremlins that may try to dampen your creative confidence with words like 'You don't have time for this', 'There's too much to do', 'I'm just not a creative person' or 'That's not realistic' (See Section 1.3).

5.1 Turning off the evaluator and letting your ideas flow

Have you ever been with a group of people trying to think up an idea and, when anyone suggests one, someone else says why it can't possibly work? Before you know it, there are no ideas left that haven't been squashed and the mood of the group is deflated. No-one even bothers with a new suggestion because all the problems have arisen before it gets uttered. Similarly, when you're on your own, have you found you can't think of a solution to a problem without coming up with all the reasons why it won't work? If you want to stop a process of creating new ideas, there's no better way than to divert mental energy to evaluating each one as it comes up. Try

Take the brakes off and set your creativity free

it out. Evaluation creates hesitation in the free flow of generating ideas and takes energy away from creative thinking. At its worst, evaluation creates a fear of getting it wrong, making a fool of yourself, of failing. When those pressures are on you, your imagination becomes

stifled, and the door slams shut on the world of dreams, possibilities, ideas and options. Lost are moments of inspiration, improvisation, surprise, intuition and the possibility that what seemed ridiculous at first may have a grain of possibility within it.

Walt Disney recognised this problem in creating films. He realised that really imaginative thinking often got limited by worries about the cost and questions about practicalities. He came up with a solution: he separated out the processes of dreaming (imagine what if…?), of being a realist (how could that work?) and being a critic (why would we?). The realist and critic bit is for other chapters – that's when you bring in questions about goal setting and values. That's the time for judgement and practicalities. The point here is to recognise you need to allow time for your creative explorer to generate as many possibilities and ideas as you can, regardless of what's realistic. In the words of Dr Linus Pauling, who incidentally is the only person to have been awarded two unshared Nobel prizes (Chemistry and Peace), 'The best way to have a good idea is to have a lot of ideas.'

That might sound like a crazy proposition, indeed a waste of time. Why bother coming up with ideas that you 'know' won't work? The first reason is, some apparently impossible ideas have happened – landing a space explorer on Mars, winning the X Factor, running 100 metres in under 10 seconds, the Paralympics. Second, there's also a lot to learn from the impossible. The 'impossible' – the out there, the curve-ball, the trip, the off-centre – may just have something in it, a kernel of something that, if you build on it, may lead to other options and ultimately to the solution you're looking for. Finally, often the best ideas come from combinations of different ideas, so letting all the ideas 'out there' might allow new combinations to form that will hit the nail on the head.

How to allow time for your creative explorer

The principle here is that to allow the creative processes to happen, you need to let go of evaluation by planning dedicated time for the creative space. How to do that can depend on the context, yet keeping the principle in mind can go a long way.

First of all, recognise that allowing time to 'create' may save time and energy in the long run.

Second, give yourself permission to have creative time – time for ideas and for dreaming – knowing that there will be time for evaluation later on. That time will vary. This could be planning how you manage a few hours. For example, if you have two hours set aside to start a piece of coursework, perhaps spend 20 minutes of 'playtime' at the start to see what comes out. Or it might be how you conduct a meeting with a society: perhaps for a one-hour meeting to discuss the next extravaganza party, you set aside 25 minutes to creatively explore the possibilities, suspending any evaluation during that process. Or, at the start of an exam answer, you might spend the first 5 minutes allowing ideas to flow. You could also build up a routine – a habit – of creative time each morning or when it suits.

Third, follow a simple rule which is ideas can only be added to. You can only offer a new idea or add to an existing idea, you can't take away. To keep your ideas flowing during this time it's useful to 'watch your language' to keep your evaluator quiet, whether you're on your own or with others. Avoid words that shut things down like 'but', 'no', 'yeah but', 'can't', 'no way', 'never', 'impossible', 'wrong', 'won't work because' .... Instead use words like 'how about ...?'. 'what if ...?'. 'yes', 'and ...'. Note: It might be helpful to note that when creating ideas, there's no commitment. None of the ideas are going to come to fruition if you don't want them to. After you've finished being creative, you can bring back the evaluation in the way you want to before deciding on the best ways forward (see diagram on the following page).

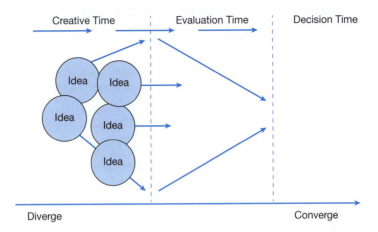

5.2   Ideas Generator – stimulating fresh possibilities

How often have you heard someone say, 'I was really stuck, so I sat at my desk and thought really, really hard while staring at the screen, and suddenly it came to me'? OK, so you might be in a more imaginative space at the desk, surfing the internet to take you somewhere else. Fair enough **Imagine what it's like being a hedgehog** if that works for you. More often you hear people say things like, 'It was weird, I was in the supermarket and saw the bread being stacked up and I realised ....'. Or, 'I was cycling home last night and it suddenly dawned on me that ...'. In the supermarket, on your bike, on the golf course, taking a walk, lying awake at 2.00 am, watching a film – these kinds of situations are so often when the ideas that count emerge. Sometimes the harder you try to be creative, the less creative you feel.

How to stimulate the flow of ideas

Taking a different perspective can be a helpful way to help stimulate different ideas. You might call this something like 'provoking insights from random association' or a 'perspective generator'.

This follows three stages:

First pick something random to stimulate your thinking (object, memory, place).

Second, ask yourself 'What does this make me think of and how does it make me feel?'

Third, your answer to the last question is a perspective from which to look at your topic. Ask yourself, 'When I look at my topic from this perspective, what possibilities does this create?'

Fourth, repeat this process to create more perspectives. You can also combine them. When you've a range of perspectives you'll have created a range of ideas. You can then look across these to create more ideas still. (If this feels a bit strange then it may be helpful to know that the more you provoke yourself to explore pathways of thinking that you least use the more creative you can become.)

For example, I want to think of ideas for a dissertation. I'm outside and see a 'hedgehog' (Step 1). Hedgehogs remind me of cars going too fast and I feel sad (Step 2). When I think of my dissertation it makes me think of ideas around driving, risk, nature, protected species (Step 3).

Another example. I want to improve my essay marks. I love football and am watching the World Cup. I watch a save from a goal keeper and it reminds me how I'm always defensive, not taking any risks. When I think of my essays I start to look at what it might be like to be more 'attacking'.

Take your topic and try this with a number of random associations to see what different perspectives you can create and how many ideas you can generate. You can use anything, for example:

Favourite film	Best holiday	A sport
Laughter	Cartoon character	Spaceman
Monk	Leisure	A garden plant
A drink	An animal	Poet

Tip: you can also create different perspectives by following a theme: for instance different players or positions in a sports team; different instruments of an orchestra or different styles of music, different bands; different colours, different types of food, meals or regions of food.

Thinking creatively about your dissertation

Students sometimes feel stuck with their dissertation. You might not have a clue what to do it on. You might know what to do it on but not know how to take it forward. It might feel quite precious, with so much at stake for your degree and your career … Imagine a student stuck in front of their computer. Stuck is the word. Can't find any inspiration. Then imagine the student goes for a walk in a nearby wood. In the wood they start to play with different perspectives: 'A time when I was inspired', 'Grey Squirrels', 'My best ever holiday', 'My favourite film star', 'Windsurfing', 'Trees' (since one was there!). Think how the student might spend time with each one to create ideas:

'When I was inspired' reminds her of when she first came across her subject and how it opened her eyes to the details of how things work. Could the dissertation look into such detail to really get at how something works?

'Grey Squirrels' reminded her of all the notes she'd got hoarded away since A-Levels: could she look back over old notes to remember what was interesting to her at different times?

'My best ever holiday' was when she had lots of friends with different interests doing different things: could she think of a wider group of people she could be with in her dissertation? Perhaps a placement somewhere or working with a group in some way?

'My favourite film star' turned out to be a heroine. She played a role that …

'Windsurfing' led to being in the outdoors, the changeable weather…

From a 'Trees' perspective she saw something strong, steady and deep-rooted …

5.3 Creating from more of your senses and intuition

A clue to getting creative about being creative lies in the ways we often hear students describing being stuck, for example, 'I've run out of ideas', 'Can't see what to do next', 'Don't know which way to turn', 'Not sure how to get over this', 'Nothing chimes for me', 'Doesn't ring true', 'Can't make it work', 'Can't spot the way forwards' and of course, simply, 'I'm stuck'. The words used point to 'being stuck' as a sensory experience – run, see, ring, turn, spot. The odd thing about university is how it often encourages students to inhabit a head space dominated by language and logic. That may be OK to a point, but when you get stuck and want fresh ideas then remaining in that headspace can be a real blocker. Imagine

Tickle your senses and make your imagination laugh

what might happen if you broaden your creative side to include things that are more visual, bring in movement, use drawing, add music and more to create a rich sensory experience in which ideas can emerge and intuitive gut feelings can be expressed. How different this may be to sitting at a desk, holding a discussion in a meeting room or getting around the table to talk it over. As history has shown these are unlikely settings to stimulate those Eureka moments.

Our intuition 'speaks' in all sorts of ways: body language, dreams, emotions, hunches, gut feelings. It can be hard to put into words 'It just feels right', can be difficult to trust. It can appear irrational, illogical, spooky, off the wall, even! And yet, intuition can be the very source of the creative inspiration we need. The question is: Can we encourage such

moments to jump out? For 40 years Charles Darwin lived at Down House where part of the grounds included 'The Sand Way'. This became his 'thinking path'. The story goes that as a child he was encouraged to walk and think; as an adult Darwin continued this habit and walked his thinking path for five circuits each day at noon, with his dog of course, each time laying down a small flint to remind him of how many circuits. He stopped to look at flowers, hear bird song, touch leaves and take in smells. Many of his ideas are said to originate from these walks. You could say being creative evolves naturally when you select the best pathways.

How to get beyond your mind

The principle here is to broaden your creative thinking space by involving more of your senses to help generate ideas and be more intuitive. The more you challenge yourself to explore using the senses that you use the least, the more creative 'edge' it can give to your experience and then the more novel your ideas may become. We've set this out as a menu of ideas from which you can choose and then apply creatively in a way that works for you. As you experiment with these try them out with a real topic, one where you want to generate some fresh ideas. For example, how to conclude an essay, manage finances, revise more effectively, cope socially, get healthier, what to do after university.

Metaphor. Intuition is sensed in non-verbal ways, which is one reason it can seem tricky to articulate. Have a go at expressing whatever you're thinking by using images and metaphors that pop into your mind. For example 'As I thought of that it was like snowflakes landing on a roof' or 'That idea made me feel like I'm flying through turbulence' or 'The answer seems to be like a bowl of fresh fruit'.

Using your body. Go for a walk and walk in the way that feels most like being stuck. Then walk in different ways – sideways, backwards, fast, slow, stop, start, hop, skip – see what emerges. Trust your intuition and blurt out whatever comes to mind. You could do the same with dance, yoga, sports moves. You could also try being different statues: become a statue that physically expresses what you're experiencing emotionally. For example, if feeling confused then be a confused statue. Then physically change your body shape and posture to create different statues to see what feelings and ideas emerge.

Pictures. Draw a picture of being stuck, then one of being unstuck. Create a story board of pictures between the two to represent ways forwards. What ideas lie behind the pictures?

Images. Find or create images that represent being stuck and unstuck. You could use magazine cutouts to create the pictures, take some photographs, or make a physical model.

Music. Play or listen to music or songs. Create a playlist that stimulates a creative journey from where you are now to where you want to be with all the possibilities and ideas that emerge on the way.

Gut feeling. Tune into your body and literally say what you're feeling at that moment. Say the first thing that comes to mind no matter how ridiculous it seems. For example 'I feel all hot and prickly when I think about it that way', or 'Hearing that idea makes my stomach churn' or 'My tummy tingles at the thought of going down that road'. Over time you'll discover more about what these sensations are telling you and learn to trust your 'gut feeling'.

Tip: Whatever senses you experiment with try saying the first thing that comes into your mind at each stage, however ridiculous it may sound. It may end up being off the mark but until you let it out there you'll never know.

5.4 Creating creative conversations

One story of being creative tells it as a somewhat lonely affair. Think of Newton and the apple, the scientist in the lab, the composer at the piano, the artist in the studio. History is littered with stories of individuals who apparently solved problems or created inventions through their own self-determined genius. Such histories are rarely accurate, for they tend to hide the conversations and relationships through which the particular individual became attributed with an idea. When it comes to creative thinking there's a risk of assuming that this is all down to you, waiting for your genius-inspired moment. In the other sections of this chapter we've not made much mention of the role that others can play in bringing out your creativity. However, every factor that stimulates your creativity increases tenfold and more if you bring others into the equation.

Working with other people to create ideas seems such an obvious point, hardly worthy of a section in itself. Time and time again, however, we work with students who spend their time trying to resolve something on their own, never realising that a creative conversation with a peer, a friend, a family member or someone at work might provide just the **When it comes to being creative, the more the merrier!** input they need. And time and time again we also work with groups of people, including students, though also professors and people from other walks of life, who when they get together to explore some possibilities, fall at the first hurdle by letting their evaluation heads come into play all too early. Working creatively together does seem to require paying some attention to create a cross-fertilisation of ideas and divergent thinking.

How to work with others creatively

The principle here is creating creative conversation, and though we're focused on how you might work with others to help you develop ideas, the principles apply equally to when you're working more formally in a team.

Take the topic you want to get creative about, and bearing in mind the tools from the other sections of this chapter:

First, think about who to speak to. Include people who may not be obvious. For example, explaining the challenges you're facing with an essay to someone who has no clue about it, may lead to some questions you'd completely overlooked asking yourself. For example, if you're doing science, bring in an artist, social scientist, statistician, musician.

Second, think about where would be good to have a 'freeing up' conversation. If meeting physically, talking in a café, playing sport, meandering round a gallery, or walking outside might prompt new ideas. If on the phone you might want to be moving while you converse.

Third, agree the rules, namely, not to allow the evaluator into the conversation. The aim at this point is to enable as many ideas to emerge as possible. What's needed is a spirit of curiosity. Now is the time for listening with openness, without judgement and with curiosity so you can give ideas and possibilities the freedom to emerge without putting up barriers. That will require communicating in ways that encourage, that show respect, and that build on and add to. For example, 'That's interesting, tell me more' and 'I'd never have thought of that' and 'What about if ...' will all help.

You and your relationships – making them work

Relationships play a big part, an emotional part, in shaping your university experience. You're in a relationship with your lecturers, your peers, other people in your university, potential employers, your friends, family and with others in your life. Why stop there? You're in a relationship with yourself and your emotions as well as with the degree itself. Not to mention your relationships with time, money, food, computers, alcohol. The university experience is full of relationships.

- What do your relationships say about you?
- When do you need to be more honest?
- How would better relationships transform your university experience?

At times those relationships work well: lecturers engage with your study, peers offer support, you get on with your flatmates, there are clubs and societies you feel part of, you've exciting relationships with new friends, have a flourishing social life, and you feel good about yourself and your relationship with your degree. Sometimes, however, relationships become

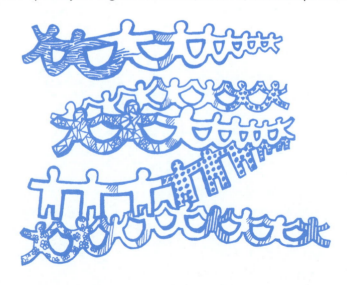

a hindrance: relationships with lecturers can feel awkward, your peers can feel over-competitive or not interested in you, you can feel very alone or not alone enough in a new environment, you don't have the confidence to talk about your study to others, your subject doesn't seem relevant to anything in the world, the stress of it all has led you to retreat from social life, you don't feel in touch with yourself anymore and your relationship with your university life is one of angst.

> This chapter is about how you form and transform in the way that you want to. We experience relationships which are fundamental in shaping your university.
>
> We are inviting you to explore:
> - Emotional wisdom – managing your relationship with emotions
> - The Emergent Relationship – identifying what your significant relationships need from you
> - Managing misunderstanding – sharing expectations
> - Confronting confrontation – lowering the risk

> Students say when relationships aren't going well it's like ...
> ... depressing ... lonely ... feel pathetic as a squid ... abrasive ... chalk and cheese ... formal ...draining ... blowing hot and cold ... sparks flying ... lukewarm ... stormy ... fiery ... tit for tat ... singing out of tune
>
> Students describe relationships going well as like ...
> .... not thinking about it ... smooth ... harmonious ... two peas in a pod ... in an open-top car on a sunny day ... a rainbow ... sitting by the fire ... birdsong ... walking arm in arm ...

Note: we want to re-emphasise the point that your relationships are not just with other people. They include your relationship with yourself and your emotions as well as with things around you. Think how angry people get at objects like computers that crash, at junk emails, at the car that won't start, at the bike tyre with a puncture, at noise. And what about 'the degree' itself, as something you have a relationship with? Taking responsibility for the relationships you're in and for how you are within them is an important part of your evolving emotional wisdom. This starts with being aware of how your emotions influence your words, behaviours, actions and decisions and how you can use this awareness in forming better relationships.

Topics in other chapters also play a part here – after all, they all contribute to your emotional wisdom. For your relationships to be what you want them to be, you need to have a clear sense of what you value (Section 1.2) and to be aware of any interrupting Gremlins that throw doubt on what's possible (Section 1.3). Your relationships could benefit by considering the balance in your university experience (Section 7.5). They may need you to have clearer goals and a steadier focus. Perhaps they need you to be more confident. Indeed, you may need to apply some creative thinking to your relationships. The important thing is to recognise that, in all these areas, relationships are a key piece of the jigsaw, and that 'how you are' is a key part of the relationships you're in. Finally, in the exercises we present here, being aware of what is in this moment for you is important – some of the mindfulness exercises in the final chapter can help in tapping into what is in this moment.

Just thinking about relationships and emotions may feel a bit heavy. It doesn't have to be. It can be hugely rewarding and liberating to pay attention, learn and understand more about your relationships. Watch out for any Gremlins that are trying to make dealing with emotions and relationships more difficult than needs be (See Section 1.3).

6.1 Emotional wisdom – managing your relationship with emotions

Students often talk of their relationship with their university experience as one of ups and downs. A shifting emotional landscape of excitement, boredom, overwhelm, joy, fear, sadness, happiness, envy, guilt, surprise, nervousness, pleasure, anxiety, depression, hatred, sorrow, delight, peace, and more. Some emotions seem to stick around a bit longer, others seem to come and go. One moment all is well – you've had great feedback on an essay or discovered a new club – and the next it all falls apart as a best friend lets you down or you run out of money. We're sure you can add more examples here.

Being in tune with your emotions is the first step

The question is, how are your emotions shaped by and shaping the relationships you're in? Awareness and understanding of your emotions, and the emotions of others is part of your growing 'emotional wisdom'. Emotional wisdom also means being able to make choices based on that awareness by taking responsibility for how you're being, and how you're impacting on other people.

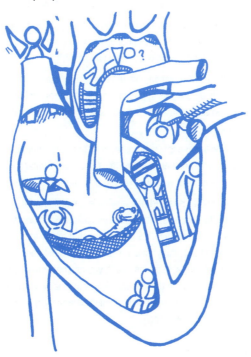

How to bring your emotional wisdom into play

Becoming more aware of your emotions in a situation means you can start to see how they impact not just on what you feel, but also on how you think, behave, how you come across, what you say and how you listen. Greater awareness of other people's emotions and your assumptions about them also helps to see how these are affecting you. You can use a past situation to explore this, and then, in hindsight, imagine how different it would've been if you'd been more aware of your emotions and managed your response to them differently.

Step 1. Take a relationship and think of a recent interaction with that person which didn't go as well as you'd have liked. Bring it alive:

- What were you talking about? What were you wearing? What could you see? What could you hear? What would somebody watching you have seen?
- What emotions were you experiencing? What were you feeling physically?
- What emotions were you aware of or assuming in the other person?

Step 2. Next, ask, 'How were my emotions affecting my body language, what I was saying, what I was thinking, how I was behaving and how I was coming across?' And 'How were my emotions either helping or hindering me in this situation?'

Step 3. Then, ask, what would you like to have experienced? How might relating or responding with your emotions have changed how you were physically, how you thought, what you did, what you said and how you said it?

Step 4. Now re-enact the interaction, this time with your more helpful approach to your own emotions. How does this approach change how you feel physically, how you think, what you do, what you say and how you say it? What's different before, during and after the interaction?

Step 5. Finally, how will you apply your learning from this to future interactions in a specific relationship? What do you want for this relationship, what's your intention? What, given greater emotional wisdom, will you do differently in future interactions?

Experiencing strong emotions is part of a normal life. Watch out for any judgement about your emotions, for example, automatically thinking emotions like anger or frustration are necessarily negative. It's the actions that follow that you may want to evaluate, rather than the feeling itself. If you can be honest about the emotion you're experiencing, and are able to observe it, you can become more aware of your response to the emotion and the choices that follow in what you do. Indeed, when the 'energy' of an emotion is observed and channelled differently, even what may feel like 'bad' emotions can become enabling.

Tip: for some people, emotions have a connection to colours. As the artist Pablo Picasso is said to have remarked, 'Colours, like features, follow the changes of the emotions.' You can bring colour to the above exercise in how you describe your emotions. For example, you might describe 'sadness' as blue or grey, or something different. You could then paint the emotional landscape of the interaction and then play with changing the colours. Try more dilute, more intense, pastel or new colours altogether. As you change colours how do emotions change. What does this say about how you would adjust your emotions? If not colours you could be creative with sounds or shapes.

Words often used to describe emotions:

Bitter	Envious	Humble
Thrilled	Frustrated	Euphoric
Fearful	Desperate	Hostile
Angry	Lonely	Miserable
Delighted	Terrified	Horrible
Helpless	Captivated	Frustrated
Disgust	Guilty	Dejected
Cautious	Hateful	Brave
Spiteful	Shameful	Sorrowful
Love	Shocked	Other

6.2   The emergent relationship – what the relationship needs from you

When it comes to relationships in your university life it's all too easy to get caught up in a 'blame game'. After all, when things aren't going well, there are lots of things at which or whom you can point the finger: your lecturers aren't giving you good feedback or don't appreciate what you're going through, the peers around you aren't interested in your topic, your friends let your down or don't seem to care, your girlfriend or boyfriend doesn't understand the pressure you're under, your lecturers don't explain things clearly enough, those at home expect too much, your phone keeps crashing, Facebook has too many messages. Sometimes you might be quite justified in your response to all this. The question is: How well does your response help you? And, how well does it help the relationship?

> **The relationship is more than the sum of its parts**

   Managing relationships isn't just about the difficult ones. You might be really excited to have found a new connection, someone who you can share ideas with. Yet how do you keep that spark alive, how do you make space for it in a busy schedule? Perhaps you're wanting to rekindle an old relationship that you really value but for which 'life' and the degree has got in the way. What does that relationship need to keep it going? Or, maybe you find yourself in a tricky situation with a relationship that you have to engage with, and yet which feels really dysfunctional. What can you do to make it more productive? Whether this be with lecturers, peers, partners,

friends or family, or even equipment, money, time or food, sometimes it can be hard to see just what you could do to make a difference.

When you think of relationships you naturally think of yourself and of the other people involved. Yet, what of the relationship itself and its perspective? What if you also bring into account what it knows and what it needs? What if you explore your role in relation to what the relationship needs?

How to see the relationship's perspective

When you think of your friends it can feel different being with them in a group compared with being with one of them on their own. Similarly sports teams, community groups, orchestras or online groups have a collective feel beyond the contribution of any one individual. The relationship has a quality that emerges as something different and more than the sum of the individuals that are a part of it. Taking this perspective of the relationship as an entity itself offers useful insight for strengthening relationships.

Choose a relationship that you care about and that you want to improve. That doesn't mean it's a relationship that you necessarily like but it does need to be a relationship that you're committed to doing something about.

Create a triangle in which you can sit or stand and use the three corners as separate positions. Leave a couple of metres distance between each. One position is you, one position the other person and the third position is the relationship itself.

First, in your position, imagine the other person is facing you from their position. Imagine telling them what it's like for you being in this relationship. You could choose a recent interaction to get more specific, or talk more generally. Tell them how you feel, what it is that bothers you, how things look from your point of view, how you see their behaviour, what it is you want from this relationship.

Now, step away from this position and 'shake off' being you. Move into the position of the other person and step into their shoes – imagine being them! See the world through their eyes. Stand or sit how they stand. Be like them, copy their mannerisms. How do they feel? What's bothering them? How do things look for them in this relationship? What do they see you doing? How do they describe your behaviour? What pressures are they under? What do they want from the relationship? Note: it may take some practice to see the world through the other person's eyes. If you slip back into the position of being you then start this part again – try not to confuse the two perspectives.

Next, 'shake off' being them and move to the third position. This is the relationship itself, emergent from the two people in the other two positions. Imagine the relationship as a living entity, with feelings, opinions, needs. What's it like to be this relationship? Is it smooth, edgy, hot, cold, fragmented, sharp, joyful, noisy, exciting, frightening, vulnerable, strong? What does the relationship see you and the other person doing? How does it describe your behaviour? And three key questions to ask:

- What can this relationship see that the two people in the other positions can't?
- What does the relationship know that they don't know?
- What does the relationship want and need from the two people in order to move in a more positive direction?

To finish, 'shake off' and come back to your first position. Ask: what's new here that I didn't see or know before? What do I need to do, think, feel or say differently to help move this relationship onto a better footing? How do I need to be?

To take responsibility for moving this forward now set your intention for this relationship and commit to the specific steps you need to take to achieve it.

Tip: you can do this exercise with relationships to 'things'. It sounds strange and yet is very powerful to imagine the second position as something: your phone, the 'university', your flat, your 'degree', money, food, Facebook, alcohol, or drugs. You can try it out by putting the 'thing' in the second position and then in the third position your relationship with the thing. The questions remain the same!

Student experience – Sara

Close relationships can sometimes be the hardest to take a step back from. Sara had found herself annoyed about a friend:

"I applied the relationship exercise to a situation with a friend, where I was annoyed at a situation that happened around my birthday. I was feeling annoyed as my friend did not make any effort to spend time with me or even visit me on my birthday.

By using the exercise I took myself out of the situation and put myself in their shoes. From this perspective it was apparent the other person had very little time to dedicate to seeing me because of their degree and extra activities they are involved in. From the perspective of my friend, I was also seen not making an effort with our relationship. The next part of the exercise involved looking at the relationship as an outsider, and it was apparent that the relationship was distant, fragmented and awkward at times. However it could be seen there was potential for it to be a good friendship like it was in the past.

By carrying out the exercise it made me realise that although I was annoyed at the person, I was seeing the situation as an act of rudeness or lack of caring, but in fact it probably was due to other pressures acting on that person. After the exercise, I have realised that more effort needs to be put into the friendship from both sides. From my side I am going to try and invite the person to more events and also take more of an interest in their activities. I also learnt that I may need to be more understanding about situations and not be so quick to judge."

Student experience – Ruth

It can be hard to find your independence at university. Ruth was struggling to find a new way of relating to her mum:

"I was finding the way my mum was acting very difficult to deal with, I felt she was being over-protective, making it very difficult for me to do the things I wanted to, or at least with a great deal of guilt on my part. It was making me feel resentful. When Will walked me through this exercise it was over the issue of me going backpacking, my mum felt that as a lone female the idea was ridiculously dangerous and that she needed to stop me from going.

As you can tell from above my whole thought process was based on what I was feeling/doing/wanting with very little perspective as to why my mum was acting the way she was. Without understanding the why it was very difficult to empathise and be able to offer a solution that could work for both of us.

Will got me to use space to work through our relationship, placing myself at one point in the room, me pretending to be my mum at another. By physically moving between the points I was literally shifting perspective between my own and my mum's, at each point asking questions such as: How does it feel where I am? Why does it feel like this? Where do I want to get to? How can I get there?

Remembering that at one point I am myself and at the other I am my mum, it encouraged me to think through a different perspective, to think through her objections rather than just glossing over them as annoying, or letting them get to me.

Answering each of these questions out loud, rather than in my head was important, even if it felt a little weird, it makes what each 'person' in the scenario is saying real, more tangible rather than something I just made up.

Once I realised why my mum was acting the way she was, she was scared for me and wanted to stop bad things from happening to me, it became easier to plan a conversation that would address her fears but one in which I could remain calm and in control to stop things descending into another argument which solved nothing and only made things worse."

6.3 Managing misunderstanding – sharing expectations

All too often, misunderstanding, bad feeling or even conflict arises from a lack of clear expectations between people. What may seem obvious to you is not necessarily obvious to someone else. What you mean by tidying up may be very different to your flat mates' or partner's definition. And, think of words like regular, soon, clean, respect, fun, quiet, support, taking turns, sharing, love, honesty, trust, truth. You might agree all of these with someone, though each of you could have a very different understanding about what the words mean in practice. Perhaps you've agreed with a friend to respect each other's opinions, yet do you have a shared notion of what respect looks like and what sorts of behaviours that entails? Or maybe

Real understanding requires generosity

you've agreed with your partner, parents or children that they support you during a tricky part of your degree? Have you agreed explicitly what that support will involve and specifically what they need of you in return?

It's surprisingly unusual for people to have real conversations about their relationships and expectations of each other. It can seem easier to put these off or avoid them altogether. Sometimes referred to as 'doorstep' disclosures where the real issue is only raised as the person is leaving and there's an easy way to 'exit' if it feels too tricky. These conversations can take courage. At the same time you can also hold them in a way that makes the space feel safer and more constructive.

How to share and respect expectations

While the principle here is straightforward, we do know that conversations about relationships can feel awkward. Awkwardness in the short term can however save a lot of discomfort in the long term. Here we offer a way of holding an open and honest conversation about expectations within a space of 'fair play'. By sharing in this way, something new can be learnt about what's needed to take the relationship forward and then an agreement established. If a conversation like this feels out of the question or feels too risky then the next section (6.4) offers an alternative approach.

Choose a relationship where it feels OK for each of you to talk honestly about what you each want and need. Decide where to have this conversation: an informal chat while walking on the beach, during a car journey, over a coffee or a beer, in the park?

First, agree that you're both going to:

- Take turns – share your thoughts in a fair and balanced way.
- Not argue or be defensive – speak and listen with compassionate honesty and without being judgemental.
- Not rely on telepathy! – be real, say it as it is.

Second, now, decide who's going to start then take turns in speaking about expectations, do one at a time using the following structure:

- My request – 'What I expect from you is …' and My assumption – 'What I think you expect from me is …'. Then swap.

Third, once you've identified some key expectations, work out the detail, ask, 'What does that look like in practice?' What are the behaviours needed to fulfil that expectation?

Finally, use what you've both discovered to agree on how you'll act and be together in this relationship.

The outcome will be work in progress, so you don't need to look for a finished product. Actually, great value comes from keeping this as something to explore and update as part of the ongoing relationship.

Tip: you might find being more playful can help in having such a conversation. Perhaps you could create a game in which you each write your expectations on some cards and then play Snap! Or try it with story-telling, music, drama, pictures, rhymes, rhythms.

Note: it's likely that making a deal with a work colleague would be different to one with a partner or friend. Similarly, how trusting – or otherwise – you are of the person may affect how explicit this conversation is. You may, for example, choose to cover only practicalities like who does what and when and to leave out more intimate emotional and/or physical needs. The key here is using the underlying principle about sharing expectations. With a bit of imagination you can use this principle even if the other person is tricky to talk with. For example, while walking to a meeting you might weave expectations into the conversation.

6.4   Confronting confrontation – lowering the risk

There's sometimes a need for a conversation that you would rather not have to have. The sort of conversation where what you need to say feels too risky or confrontational. Perhaps you fear hurting the

Whether you say it or not, it will still be there

others persons feelings? Perhaps you fear it will expose your vulnerability? Or perhaps you fear the consequences because you don't know where it will lead? This could be a conversation with a friend, another student, a lecturer, a boyfriend, girlfriend, brother, sister, boss, parent. The topic could be anything from how you feel let down, to finance, essay marks, lack of trust, unacceptable behaviours, booking a holiday, saying no, facing a hard truth, what to do at the weekend. Sometimes even a trivial subject can feel confrontational and seem explosive.

 Check in case your Gremlins are blowing things out of proportion. And even if they're right and there's a big problem, you certainly don't want them directing the conversation. There's nothing more exhausting than a conversation with your Gremlins trying to reason with someone else's! (See Section 1.3)

How to lower the risk in confrontation

The principle is that with the right preparation, by sticking to some ground rules and by following a planned structure, you can lower the risk of a potentially confrontational conversation. Preparation means you can be clear on what you need to say and also work out how to say it in a way that is neither aggressive nor defensive. The key is to be succinct and avoid judgement by taking the heat out of your words.

For preparation, set out a 60-second opening statement to the conversation. Own your words by saying 'I' or 'For me' rather then we, them, us. Perhaps write it down. This needs to include:

- Naming the issue clearly
- A specific example that illustrates the situation or the behaviour that you feel needs addressing
- How you feel about the issue
- What you think is at stake
- What you see as your contribution to the issue
- An explicit indication that you want to resolve it
- That you want to hear the other person's response

As part of preparation take some time to get in a useful state of mind (see anchoring, Section 4.1), and pay particular attention to your 'emotional wisdom' (see Section 6.1).

Step 1. To start the conversation, take a few deep breaths then begin by voicing your 60-second opening. Keep it brief, stick to time! Then be quiet, staying in the state of mind you've chosen.

Step 2. Now Listen. Be curious about the other person. Your job is to actively listen. Keep an open mind, suspend your own judgements, avoid being defensive and respect what they're saying. Avoid finding fault or apportioning blame. You're trying to learn what it's like for them.

Step 3. Once they have spoken, ask questions to clarify what they mean. Paraphrase back to make sure you've understood. Let them know that you've understood their position, what they're saying and what's important for them.
Keep a slow pace, allow silence.

Step 4. Assess together what is being learned. Have you left anything unsaid? Is there anything the other person has left unsaid? Has the elephant in the room found its voice?

Step 5. Finally, seek common ground and agreement. Where does this put both of you now? What's required to move forward? Aim to make an agreement about the next steps that each of you will take.

Note. Sometimes it's still difficult to reach an agreement; then the interim arrangement is to seek third-party mediation.

Too many setbacks? Call forth your resilience whatever happens

Doing a degree, indeed university life in general, can feel like a rollercoaster at times. One minute you're up, feeling over the moon, the next you're down, carrying the weight of the world on your shoulders. There are so many things lined up waiting to knock you down: endless reading lists, coursework lining up, unfamiliar surroundings, poor marks received, realising your overdraft is at the limit, problems at home, friends placing unfair demands, illness, receiving bad news, career options closed down. How do you respond to all those things? How resilient are you to the many, many challenges and setbacks you'll face?

The good news is your resilience is independent of what life throws at you and can even be strengthened by how you learn to respond to all those challenges and setbacks. People call forth their resilience in the most extreme situations, including disasters, wars and famine. This is the choice we raised in the beginning of

- How do you want to be in the face of setbacks?
- Who are you being when your resilience is strong?
- What do you gain by worrying?

the book i.e. choosing 'how you will be' in the face of whatever setbacks appear to stand in your way. Setbacks are of course an inevitable part of doing a degree and of life generally. Stuff happens. What doesn't need to be inevitable is how you respond.

Responses come in many forms. They can include how you interpret a situation, what you do in a situation as well as how you are in that situation. It may mean making some distance, finding depth, easing off the pressure, evening out the pace, going with the flow, staying true to your values, remaining resourceful, being light, keeping curious or learning.

 It's tough when the pressure is on and can feel like nothing else is possible. 'Everything is against me', 'It's so unfair', 'Why me?', 'Poor me', 'There's no choice'. These are the voices – the moods – of the Gremlins; they rarely help you respond in a resilient way (See Section 1.3).

 In a way, all of this book plays a part in building your resilience. Resilience is not something that stands alone – resilience comes from having strong foundations. Part I gives you those foundations, the deep roots to hold you steady when things get tough, roots that need looking after. These roots hold you true to your values, keep your sense of purpose and direction steady. The chapters in Part II add further resources, which help you develop resilience like growing new branches on a tree. Resources such as keeping confident, finding your focus, being creative, having challenging conversations. In this chapter we offer some additional 'tools' that can help when you're experiencing setbacks. These tools are based on the assumption that you've worked through the foundations of Part I as well as other chapters relevant to you from Part II. You may also find some of the tools in the final chapter helpful in becoming present. You need to find out what works for you to be resilient.

In this chapter we explore:

- Stepping back by using your imagination
- Letting go and getting going
- Reframing to shed a new light on things
- Recharging step by step
- Moving one step at a time towards a better balance
- Saying Yes by Saying No

Students say when their resilience is low it feels like …

… a deflated balloon … a sore head …trapped in a cage … heart sinking … being kicked when you're down … being picked on … a stubbed toe … a brick wall … thick mud … heavy rain … dark clouds

Students have described being resilient as like …

… I've got my walking boots on … having the power to fend off all of life's difficulties … like a professional weight-lifter … lifting the weight off my shoulders … like a tree swaying in the wind with strong roots … a lorry in the slow lane that just keeps going no matter what … being adaptable to what comes up … being prepared … like a weeble, it wobbles but never falls down...

What's it like for you when your resilience is low?
What's it like when you're being resilient?

This chapter is about allowing your resilience to be more readily available when needed. In addition we have offered ways of giving a boost to your resilience during the more difficult times, when you're under pressure. We know from working with many students that all the strategies and techniques offered in this book do work, so we hope you've made them work for you. If not, we suggest you try them again, they can take practice, and you can adapt them to find a way to make them work for you – or perhaps there are some Gremlins getting in the way that you need to deal with first?

7.1 Stepping back by using your imagination

It's easy to lose your sense of perspective when you're under pressure or when things go wrong. Things get out of proportion, seem bigger than they are, more troubling than they need be. This can be especially true as pressure mounts and even the smallest of things sets you off – the straw that breaks the camel's back, as the saying goes. Getting things out of proportion is seldom helpful.

Things look different in the morning – why wait?

What can be really helpful is to take a step back. Often the best way to find a constructive way forwards is by getting some distance from the situation. It's like a climber stepping back from the rock face to work out the best route up. Though a walk in the park might be just what you need, physically stepping back is not always an option. Another way to step back is to use the power of your imagination to make a situation feel lighter and less troubling.

Making something important lighter – like exams or a relationship – may seem counter-intuitive. 'Surely I must keep this at the forefront of my mind', 'I must fill every minute of my time with this', 'I must give it every ounce of my energy', 'I must think about this and nothing else'. Notice the Gremlins raising the stakes. Stepping back from a fire (see Section 1.3) in order not to burn can still leave you with enough heat to stay warm…

How to step back by using your imagination

Images created in your imagination have a powerful impact on how you feel and act – think of the monster under the bed, the demon behind the door, the nightmare, the tickle of a loose thread that feels like a spider. The principle here is to imagine a situation in a different way, literally exploring different mental images to see what makes it feel more helpful. For example, you might edit the image to change proportions or colours to make it feel lighter and less daunting. The following is a way to do this.

Step 1. Think about a setback, a situation where your resilience is lacking. What do you see in your mind's eye? Perhaps it's a reading list, a person, blank pages, red pen marks, a room, a ticking clock, an examiner, a crowded place, something different.

Step 2. Make the image as vivid as you can, include colours and sounds. When you concentrate on the image, how do you feel, emotionally and physically? Perhaps you're experiencing sweaty palms, excitement, fear, a beating heart, a hot flush, overwhelm, sick, heavy shoulders, freaked out, relaxed, anxious, hot under the collar, cold feet.

Step 3. Now, experiment by changing the appearance of the image in your imagination and adjusting the sounds. Pretend you're a 'video editor'. Be playful, with each edit; notice how your feelings and emotions change. Try editing the image by making it:

- Black and white
- More colourful
- Bigger
- Smaller
- Closer – zoom in until it's 'in your face'
- Further away – zoom out until a dot on the horizon
- Blurred and fuzzy
- Sharp and clear
- In a different place – move left, right, up, down, behind you
- Speed it up, slow it down, keep it still – freeze frame
- Try different sounds, for instance your favourite song or music or squeaky voice
- Change anything you like! Even add a cartoon character or something funny

Step 4. Now, based on the changes you've experienced by editing, create the image that feels most helpful. The key question is: how do you want to be with this situation that's setting you back? It might be you want to experience relaxed eyes, a gentle smile, heart not pounding, a calm determination, alertness, peace of mind, energised, standing tall, shoulders back, slower breathing or lightness. What works for you?

Step 5. Spend time 'sitting' with this image and experience the associated feelings. What will seeing and experiencing the situation in this way enable for you? What's important here? What do you need to let go of in order to move forwards?

Tip: you could also think about situations in the future that you're making unduly stressful or troubling and use the same method to take a step back from these.

Student experience – Rob

Sometimes stepping back can help get things into proportion and see what you might be able to let go of. Rob was struggling with revision:

"For this challenge I focused on one particular aspect of my degree experience, revision and exams, because I felt as though I was lacking in preparation and needed some help in regaining confidence in my ability to revise. In response to the challenge I sat in my bedroom crossed-legged on my bed and looked at my revision folder; flicking through the pages, listening to the noises of them moving through and closing my eyes, visualising some of the module title pages. In my mind the topic was making me feel quite frustrated that no information seemed to be 'going in' for my revision and I noticed my heart rate was increasing quite a lot. I was feeling a little nauseous, defeated and disappointed in myself.

I played with the pages in my mind's eye for the next step; walking around my bedroom, making module codes bigger and smaller, further and nearer as the challenge required and found myself to be smiling. Whilst no single one of the aspects the challenge asked me to use was any more important than another, a combination of them all was making me feel a lot lighter inside.

The challenge made me realise that I needed to let go of how seriously I was taking things, to take a deep breath about the whole issue and realise that exams were not the 'be-all-and-end-all' of life. By getting worked up I was only making things worse for myself. It helped in making me feel much calmer and as far as feeling resilient goes, it helped me to steel myself for more revision and the exams ahead. At the time I still had 2 weeks to go before my exams and knew that if I focused and just took a deep breath every now and again, I could get the job done. It helped in making the exam period much more bearable and enabled me to use the task in other aspects of my life; to just take a few seconds out of problematic issues and calm myself down, steeling myself for the problems ahead."

7.2 Letting go and getting going

It's amazing how much energy 'worry' can take. Worry can really grind you down. Those constant nagging thoughts that stop you switching off, keep you awake, distract you from what you're trying to do, dominate conversations with your friends. The thing about worry is it tends to focus all your attention on what might go wrong, on what you're trying to avoid or don't want to happen.

Imagine all the energy you put into thinking about what you don't want!

Sometimes the worry feels very rational – it's as if you're trying to think through all the possibilities – you're working things out, exploring all the contingencies, making sure you're prepared. To a point this may well be true. The question to ask, though, is – 'Can I stop?' Is the 'working things through' intentional or has worry taken over in disguise? Is worrying itself something you've chosen to do, or is it hanging around, going in circles, dominating your thoughts and feelings?

Worrying takes a lot of effort

Recognising 'worry' for worry is one thing. Stopping worrying is another thing all together. Here we want to offer a strategy for letting go and getting going. The challenge in this is having the wisdom to decide what's worth giving attention to, and what to let go of.

There are strategies in other chapters that can also be helpful. Sometimes, planning ahead can help give you the peace of mind in knowing that there's time to do all that needs to be done (see Section 3.1). It might be that your worry is to do with a lack of confidence. And, some of your worry might be generated by Gremlins fuelling an underlying fear (see Section 1.3). When you experience fear that is harder to pin down, some of the visualisations in the final chapter point to ways to embrace it (see Section 8.4).

How to let go and get going

When you're worried about something it can be helpful to identify what you can and can't do about it, i.e. whether or not you have any control or influence in the matter. Here we offer a way for doing just that. As you'll see it begins by writing down your worries, which in itself can help to get things off your mind.

First, make a list of all your concerns, the things that are bothering you, about your degree and university life. Examples might include: feeling tired; lack of money; writing blocks; stressed tutors; accommodation; family issues; being in a new environment; university policies; feeling isolated; not enough time; understanding the literature; experiment not working; exams; poor IT support; not knowing enough; future career.

Next you're going to separate these into those you can control and those you can't:

1   For each thing on your list ask: Do I have any control over this or can I influence it some way?' This is not a moment for in-depth analysis, your quick hunch will do perfectly! Answer yes or no.

2   For each of the things you've given a 'no', ask: 'If I can't control or influence this, does worrying about it really help me?' For now, acknowledge these as concerns and, however annoying, accept them as things you can't change. In doing this if you realise there's something, however small, you can do, then change it to a 'yes'.

3   Take the concerns you've given a 'yes' to having some control or influence over. Looking at these, what can you do? One useful purpose of worry is how it can nag you to take some action. What aren't you doing that you could be doing? What are you not taking responsibility for? What action, however small, can you take that could make a difference? Make a plan of action and commit to taking the first step.

Note: If you haven't given a 'yes' to anything on your list, double check. Are you being completely honest with yourself? Sometimes when the going is tough it can seem like you have no control over anything, you feel a victim to everything that happens. Is that really the case with everything you've noted 'no' to? Check for any Gremlins getting in the way!

Tip: another way you can do this is to draw a big circle with a smaller circle in the middle of it. Those concerns or worries you answered 'yes' to can be noted in the inner circle. Those with a 'no' go in the space between the inner and outer circle. You can also imagine placing all the 'no' answers in a balloon that you let go of, and watch it float away. Or, as the saying goes, 'pack up your troubles in an old kit bag'.

Student experience – Kate

Sometimes there are so many worries it is hard to see the wood for the trees. Indeed, you may find it helpful to reassess. Kate tried spending some time-out to assess her situation:

"This challenge involved listing my worries and concerns in my daily and university life, then categorising them in to 'able to control' vs 'unable to control'. I decided that to get the maximum effect out of this challenge I would do it in as neutral of a place as possible so I sat in a quiet spot on the university campus, away from the library, my home and my friends to try and be removed from the issues to begin with. I found myself including things on the list such as my worries about revision and exams at the time and careers planning alongside day-to-day concerns about my romantic and social relationships and not being able to be there for certain people who I wanted to be there for. Before this challenge I was starting to feel a little exasperated in my ability to do things. Certain aspects of my social life and day-to-day life felt helpless especially and as though there was nothing that I could do to move forward with my personal relationships and life.

After making the list I found it quite difficult to put each of them into the circles that the challenge asked me to and because worrying has always been a big concern for me I managed to fill both of them with lots of details. I found that in this challenge there seemed very little to begin with that fit in my 'able to control' circle however the challenge made me realise that everything has a little of something that can be influenced. I was underestimating myself and knocking myself down when there was no need to because as long as there was something that I felt I could do, then I at least could feel as though I was progressing forward with something, no matter how small. On the other hand, by letting go of the actions in the 'unable to control' section, I could feel much lighter in myself and just focus on those aspects of life which I had agency over.

I have since applied the challenge multiple times when I have felt as though I do not know how to move forward with life. I list the things that I think are problems and think about them, taking a little longer than the challenge originally asked me to, but also writing down on a separate piece of paper the problem and what I feel I can do to act on the issue. This has greatly helped since undertaking the challenge the first time in aiding me to feel capable of acting on the majority of the problems in my life. On the other hand it has also enabled me to let go of issues if I have no control over them, letting me put them to one side and come back to them at a later date to see if there is something new that I can move forward with."

Student experience – John

Sometimes it can be hard to know what to do with worries about the world at large. John found the circles exercise a useful way to work out his own influence:

"I used the 'two circles' challenge as a way of addressing my anxious feelings regarding my degree and general everyday life. I wanted to reduce stress levels in work and other situations in order to feel more comfortable and get greater enjoyment from these aspects of life. Due to my tendency to overly worry about issues that I have little or no control over and my occasional reluctance to take action on the things that I am able to influence, I found that visually dividing my concerns into two categories (what I can and cannot influence) helped me to create a plan of action and reduce free-floating anxiety. This enabled me to channel my energy into specific tasks as well as helping me to prioritise, for example by realising that writing an essay for one module was more pressing than doing reading for another at that time.

The challenge also helped me to let go of wider worries that I have, such as those relating to the whole university or global current affairs. While I maintain a strong awareness of these kind of issues I have developed a greater ability to filter out such concerns and focus on the things that I can affect. It also helped me to realise ways in which I can influence things that I previously thought to be beyond my control – for example I started to find that talking with people one on one can be an effective way of changing social attitudes.

I found that by providing myself with a tangible list of the actions available to me, completing the exercise had an empowering effect. I learned the merit of creating a plan of action and focusing my efforts on one task rather than wasting energy worrying about where to start. Now, when I start to feel worried about things I write a list of everything that is bothering me and highlight the things which I cannot alter, at least in the near future, and then, from the remaining items, work out which ones require the most immediate attention."

7.3 Reframing to shed a new light on things

Sometimes when you experience a setback all you can see is the worst in the situation, all the negatives. If you get a bad mark for your coursework you might find yourself dwelling on everything you did wrong. If you've had a bad night out with your friends, you might find yourself looking at how boring life is for you at the moment. If you spent too much money in the term, you might find yourself focusing on how hard it is to get by. As one thought leads to another it can become one big catastrophe.

When your resilience is strong you can take a different slant on things. Indeed, taking a different slant on things can be a way to boost your resilience. We don't want to send you into a debate about the merits of optimism, pessimism and the power of positive thinking. We do though want to suggest there's some value in being positive in a situation. By being positive we don't mean assuming everything will be how you want it to be. That's how positive thinking can be misrepresented and gets a bad name. Instead, by being positive, we mean you can make the most out of a situation. Things will inevitably go wrong at times. You can't change what's happened or necessarily what's going to happen. What you can change is how you view these situations and your response.

Shining a new light on things makes all the difference

It's the frame that you put around events that gives them their meaning and, just as an old picture can be put in a new frame to brighten it up, you can do the same with events that have happened or are going to happen.

How to shed a new light on things by reframing

Reframing involves changing the meaning you're giving to an experience by choosing a perspective that is more useful for you. You can use this for past events (like low exam marks) or things yet to happen (like a presentation you're worried about giving). It can take practice. In the words accredited to the inventor of the light bulb Thomas A. Edison, 'I have not failed. I've just found 10,000 ways that won't work.' That in itself is an example of reframing.

Pick an event that didn't go as well as you would have liked and which left you feeling deflated or negative. Maybe some feedback you received, a presentation you gave, some writing, an argument with a friend, partner or parent.

First, *identify the current frame*: What meaning are you making of this? What are you making this event say about you and about what's possible in the future? What are you saying the event implies about your degree? What assumptions are you making about what people are thinking about you? What assumptions about causation are you making? How much are you generalising how this event could affect other things in the future?

Second, *try some exploration*: Because this happened once doesn't make it a foregone conclusion that it will happen exactly the same again in the future. What alternative meanings exist? Try answering some of the following:

* What else could this mean?
* Who are you assuming is seeing the event in this way?
* What's there in this event or experience that could be useful?
* What is there for you to learn from this?
* What did you do well?

Third, the reframe: *choose a new frame with a meaning that will be more useful for you than the current one.* Watch out for the Gremlin that says 'only the worst case or more negative meaning is possible'. None of these meanings are true. They're all imagined perspectives and simply different ways of looking at things. So, with lurking Gremlins acknowledged, which meaning or frame will be most useful for you to take on? What do you want to choose this event to mean?

Fourth, *start taking responsibility*: Practise thinking about this new frame with its more useful meaning. Practice makes permanent and you've probably got good at repeating the more negative frame, telling the same old story, so now time to lay down some new neural pathways towards a brighter outlook.

Tip: you can also use reframing for a situation you're anticipating with some negativity, perhaps a presentation, picking up an essay mark, needing to have a difficult conversation.

Tip: if you like you can try reframing using drawings, objects or movement as a way of exploring the different frames.

Student experience – Emily

Feeling regret about what we wished we'd done can use up a lot of energy. Emily was worried she'd lost time in her second year:

"In the summer holidays between my second and third years I picked up a year-long diploma course and at the time believed that dropping one of the sports that I played at uni would give me more than sufficient time to complete the work. I really enjoyed it to start with and it wasn't too difficult either but as I got back into uni and the work started to pile up I began to look at it as a mistake; a waste of time which with my dissertation looming I was finding to be a precious resource! The time that I had gained from giving up hockey was most definitely being spent on my degree rather than the Diploma leaving me with little time when I wasn't actually working on one qualification or another, I ended up tired and stressing that I was going to fail both my degree and the diploma.

Reframing the situation I asked myself: Why am I doing the diploma? Why have I stopped enjoying doing it? How could I see it differently? How can I use this experience?

I remembered that I had chosen to take the diploma on because it was in my interests outside of uni that could also be a career path when I finish. I'd stopped enjoying it because I was trying to put too much importance on two issues, where one required far less work and was less important than the other. I had been constantly worrying about not getting the work done, so it always seemed like I was thinking about both and being less productive because of it.

I realised that I could stop seeing the situation as a struggle and start seeing it as a challenge but that I could use the experience to bring all the elements of my life (not just the work) back into perspective and give them the appropriate amount of attention they require. By realising that the diploma needed far less time and my third year more than my second I was able to stop feeling guilty about what I had previously seen as neglecting the diploma and get on with what needed to be done."

7.4 Recharging step by step

How often do you find yourself drained of mental, physical and emotional energy? How often do you find yourself doing the very things that you know will drain you? Different things drain different people. Some students feel energised by social life and drained of inspiration if they're on their own. Others feel quite the opposite. Some students feel energised by the challenge of a difficult essay, while for others the

thought makes their hearts sink. Some students enjoy keeping in touch with distant friends and families, while for others it feels like a burden or being controlled. The real problem comes when you are either unaware of what drains and what energises you, or are aware, yet don't know how to make changes. If you're already feeling drained, and then come against a further setback, that's when student life can get really tough.

Recharging one step at a time

Sometimes it's the combination of lots of small things that add up to leave you drained. Here we offer you a way to think about those things that add to your energy and those things that drain your energy. We challenge you to take small steps to rebalance and recharge.

First, create a list of things you do that are an unwanted drain on your energy. Literally think of everything, below are some examples:

Working in a poor environment	Trying too hard
Working for too long	Trying to be perfect
Trying to be better than	Feeling not as good as
Being pessimistic	Judging yourself
Pleasing friends	Regretting old failures
Pleasing people at work	Pleasing your family
Replaying old hurts	Replaying conversations in your head
Wishing things could be different	Telling untruths to yourself/others
Thinking about revenge	Blaming others

Thinking of lost opportunities	Thinking of resentments
Trying to control others	Worrying about what might happen
Staying up too late	Alcohol consumption
Arguing with people	Looking good
Thinking about how unfair things are	

(Adapted from Carol Adrienne, *The Purpose of Your Life*, 1998, p. 95)

Second, create a list of things you do, habits, which nurture and recharge you physically, mentally and emotionally. Literally think of those things that make you feel energised.

Third, pick out two things that drain you the most and two things that energise you the most. Write a three-step plan for each habit. Be creative, try something different.

Tip: you can pay attention to your habits over time to really check which ones drain or energise you. You may also find using cards a helpful way of doing this. Write all the draining habits on red cards, and the energising habits on green cards. Pick out your two most draining habits (assuming you want to do less of, or stop, these) and the two most energising habits (assuming you want to do more of these) and write a plan of action on the back. You can keep the cards with you as a reminder.

Student experience – Tom

You may find yourself ruminating over things in ways that are not productive and you may not be aware of. Tom found he had a habit of thinking pessimistically:

"Throughout my degree I'm often being overly pessimistic which seems to make me worry more. I think this has come from striving for perfection in my work and continuously analysing myself for weaknesses and flaws which I wish to improve.

I often 'catastrophise' – my mind increasingly travelling to the worst-case scenarios and extrapolating any self-perceived sub-par achievements to their absolute worst.

This leaves me feeling mentally drained and distracts me from my work. At times like this I've found exercise or some form of manual work distracts my mind and then I'm able to recharge my mental resilience and look at the situation at hand with renewed vigour.

This has led me to the conclusion that there is often little or nothing to worry about and that the 'problem' when I dwell on it is made bigger and insurmountable in my mind. Realistically, these are usually minor setbacks that can be rectified in time. Doing more physical things as a way of recharging mentally has also led to me feeling healthier and my work appears less stressful and easier to manage."

7.5   Moving one step at a time towards a better balance

Getting the right balance in student life is not as straightforward as some people think. Gone are the days where students seem to hang around with not much to do. It seems for many students, balancing the pressure of study with social life, with commitments to clubs and societies, with having to earn money to live, with keeping in touch with other friends and family, with caring responsibilities and while doing

Balance needs movement – try standing on one leg

the right thing for a secure future, is not always an easy task. For those with more spare time, it can also be really hard to get the balance right between over studying without burn-out and relaxing without feeling guilty.

   When you think of balance what does it conjure up? Perhaps you start with a set of traditional weighing scales, in which a weight is used to balance against the ingredients you're measuring? Maybe you think of an object, finely balanced, like a rock on the edge of a precipice? By contrast, picture a bird balancing on the branches of a high tree, a gymnast balancing on a high beam, or someone riding a unicycle. The balance shifts to something that involves – indeed requires – movement, however tiny that need be. Anyone who has learnt to ride a bike knows how much easier it is to balance on a bicycle when it's moving than when it's standing still. Notice also that balance, like movement, is something that we learn. As babies we don't know how to stand or walk. We have to learn through trial and error. We have to take the bumps, yet we get there in the end. In a similar way finding balance in university life is not a one-off fix, it's more fluid and requires movement and adaptation to the more bumpy bits.

 Gremlins may try to make finding balance feel difficult or undeserved – however well-disguised they are! And yet, getting the best balance for you right now may not be as far away as it seems. Sometimes it can only take a few small steps for you to feel quite different in terms of your level of satisfaction. Surprisingly, a few small steps, repeated over a period of time, may lead to a significantly different pattern (see Section 1.3).

How to take small steps to a better balance

Finding a better balance first requires taking a holistic view to see just what's in and out of balance – it's not always as obvious as you think. A way of doing this is to score your level of satisfaction in a number of areas of your life and your studies. This will help you see what's going well in addition to what's not – not all doom and gloom. And it will give you a basis for comparison over time. Second is taking small steps towards the balance you want. Small changes can make a huge difference.

The 'life balance wheel' shows nine areas of your life. Each could be divided further if you wish (e.g., money might be split to cash flow and savings).

In each area, ask, 'How satisfied am I?' at this moment in time. Give a score between 0 and 10 to reflect your level of satisfaction. 0 is low, 10 is high. With 0 in the centre of the circle, and 10 at the outer edge, draw a line across each segment to reflect your score. Go with your hunch – there's no right or wrong answer. It's about how you feel right now, a snapshot (you may feel differently tomorrow or next week). It isn't about what others think (friends, family or colleagues).

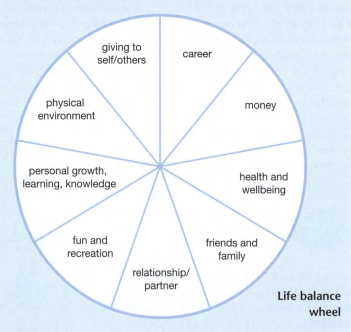

Life balance wheel

Look over the wheel as a whole. What strikes you? If you were riding a bicycle and this was one of your wheels, how would it feel? Would it be smooth? Bumpy? Hard

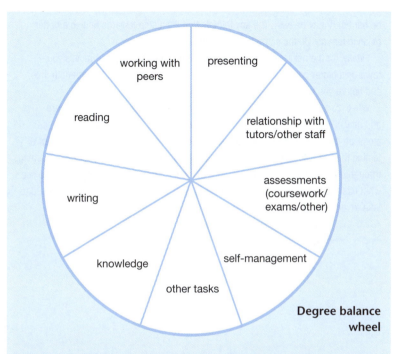

Degree balance wheel

to pedal? Note which areas stand out as needing more attention for you to feel more satisfied, to enjoy the ride more! What connections do you notice between balance and your values? What's at stake for you?

Now do the same thing for your studies using the 'degree balance wheel'. Again, give each segment a score of 0 to 10 in terms of your satisfaction. 0 is a low score, 10 is a high score. Again this is about how satisfied you feel, not what your lecturers, tutors, peers, friends, or parents think.

The segments we have suggested are open for your interpretation because different degrees involve different processes. For example, presenting might not be so important to your degree and you can replace it with something else, like practicals, or IT skills.

Then, look across the wheel as a whole. What strikes you? How would the ride feel? Note which areas need more attention for you to feel more satisfied, to enjoy the ride. Again, make connections with your values. What's really important to you about writing, for example, or what matters to you about working with peers?

From your life balance wheel, choose one of the areas where you want to improve your satisfaction score. Spend a moment working out what's missing and what would make the difference. Now commit to a small step that you could take today that would make a difference. That small step could take many different forms, and it may be hard or it may be easy. The key thing is that it's a step towards finding a better balance for you. Do the same for your degree wheel.

Finally, for the next week, commit to do something each day that moves you towards a better balance. A small step is all that is required at this moment in time, and before you know it …

While it's true that balance is something you can start to address in the here and now, it's also true that, over time, maintaining balance will require more than a one-off event. Balance in your university life will involve movement. It will involve testing the water to see what works, adapting to new demands on your time, learning through trial and error. Set a date in your diary to try the balance wheels again to see what has changed, what learning there is for you, and what further steps you need to take to maintain or improve balance.

7.6 Saying 'Yes' by saying 'No'

Sometimes a setback comes as a realisation – or perception – that you can't do all the things you set out to do. That you're human after all! You might feel over-committed or that too many demands are being asked of you. You might find it hard to say 'no' because you don't want to let someone down, or you're flattered by being asked to do something. Yet, when you say 'yes' to doing one thing, inadvertently you're also saying 'no' to something else.

Yes and no are simple words with extraordinary power

How to ... say 'yes' by saying 'no'

Saying 'yes' by saying 'no' is one way to help in finding a better balance. When you agree to do one thing, and say 'yes' to it, that means by default you're saying 'no' to something else. Flip this around. When you say 'no' to someone or to something, you're opening up the possibility of saying 'yes' to something else. In other words, saying 'no', turning things down, is not about saying 'no', it's about enabling you to say 'yes' to an alternative choice that, in this moment of time, is more important to you.

You can apply this to a decision you're faced with. Complete the following sentence:

By saying 'yes' to .... I'm saying 'no' to ....
By saying 'no' to .... I'm saying 'yes' to ....

That may be enough for you to feel stronger in what you're saying 'yes' to.
If you need to reinforce this, try:

By saying 'yes' to .... and saying 'no' to .... I'm honouring my values of ....

Tip: if you want to feel some movement with this, try walking around and repeating the sentences over and over again. Notice as you do so which feels the most resonant to you, which one feels 'right'.

Examples of saying 'yes' by saying 'no':

By saying yes to studying 12 hours a day, I'm saying no to my friendships.

By saying no to studying 12 hours a day, I'm saying yes to my friendships.

By saying no to studying 12 hours a day, and saying yes to my friendship I'm honouring my values of friendship, social life, and balance.

By saying yes to organising an event, I'm saying no to time for exercise.

By saying no to organising an event, I'm saying yes to time for exercise.

By saying no to running for an event, and saying yes to exercise I'm honouring my values of being outdoors and of health.

By saying yes to going to the night club, I'm saying no to feeling focused on revision.

By saying no to going to the night club, I'm saying yes to feeling focused on revision.

By saying no to going to the night club, and saying yes to feeling focused on revision, I'm honouring my values of achievement, discipline, satisfaction.

By saying yes to watching a late-night film, I'm saying no to Skyping home when my family are there

By saying no to watching a late-night film, I'm saying yes to Skyping home at a good time.

By saying no to watching a late-night film, and saying yes to Skyping home at a good time, I'm honouring my values of family, connections and caring.

Warning. Often things appear either/or when they are out of balance. In practice, while saying *No* in order to say *Yes* is a great way to make decisions, also look for where compromise might be possible, it does not always need to be all or nothing.

Part

III

Enjoying the Journey

Being mindful of this moment

The ethos of this book has been to encourage you to become more aware of how you can take responsibility for shaping your university experience. We've offered you various ways to experiment with different strategies to create the experience you want. Key to this experimenting has been to see what happens when you work from your 'core foundations', that is, working with a sense of vision, in alignment with your values, managing your Gremlins, recognising how you are as you set out for the day, and setting your intentions (what you are saying yes to, and what you are saying no to). Additional experiments have been offered around the themes of focus, motivation, confidence, creativity, relationships, and resilience. The word 'experiment' is important here: it's an invitation to try something out and experience something afresh. Our hope is that these experiments have helped you become more aware of yourself, your choices and the possibilities that exist for you.

We know from our experience of working with students that, while some of the exercises offer quick results and lead to 'light bulb' moments, it is not always the case, nor always desirable. Much of the emphasis of the

book has been on actively changing what you do and how you are with situations, actively putting into place strategies that will make a difference to your experience of university life. There are times, though, when too much emphasis on change can be counter-productive. Without the right attention you might find yourself striving too hard to achieve something, struggling to find a different way to be with a situation, or trying to force a change against all prevailing forces. Indeed, the very desire for change can, if you are too attached to that desire, be the source of many a problem. The desire for things to be as they were, the desire for things to be different in the future, or the desire to be like someone else, can be the very route to unrest and unhappiness. The change you had hoped for hasn't come about. The new strategies you have tried haven't had the impact you had hoped. There are things that are beyond your immediate control that continue to affect you and which you struggle to know how to deal with. Or even, you've achieved exactly what you wanted to achieve, only to find you still feel something is missing. You have new desires, there are new uncertainties and new fears or old fears re-emerging. Indeed, if you focus on change, you might find yourself losing sight of what is available to you right now.

- What is, now, right *in this moment*?
- What do you need to accept and/or let go?
- What would gratitude enable for you?

As a way to round the book up, this chapter offers some additional resources for enjoying life, even when things are not quite as you'd like them to be. To some extent it offers an antidote to feelings of disappointment or frustration when you might find yourself striving too hard, struggling to see things differently or trying to force change. At the same time, the experiments we invite you to explore here are ones that can also be used to enhance the other ideas in the book by developing further awareness and appreciation. The chapter does this by taking a different twist on the theme of change and offers a way to think about change by, rather ironically, being more aware and accepting of what is now, in this moment.

In this chapter we will explore:

- Treating this moment afresh
- Pausing to come back to the moment
- Being with your experience and letting go of the story
- Embracing fear
- Cultivating gratitude

8.1   Treating this moment afresh

A key problem in trying to enjoy the journey is when you desperately want things to be different. All the focus is on the end result, and not the journey itself. Perhaps you wish that you were on a different degree scheme, that you were living somewhere else, that you could end a relationship, be watching a different film, or not be in so much pain. It's hard to enjoy a process when you desire something else. That desire comes from focusing on what is not here, whether you're focusing on something from the past, something elsewhere or something you want in the future. While of course there are times when such comparison is useful, if our desire is so strong we have lost the ability to be in the present moment, then enjoyment is long lost. You can of course, with intention, enjoy your memories of the past, enjoy imagining being elsewhere, and enjoy dreaming of the future. That is different to being unable to experience, accept and appreciate what is in this moment because of a yearning for what is missing.

> Strive too hard and you may miss what's on offer

One step in enjoying the journey is learning to experience what is now. Sometimes the most powerful thing you can do is, well, not do, which is different to doing nothing! Please don't read this as an excuse to put off your studies or procrastinate further. Non-doing doesn't mean doing nothing. Doing nothing is suggestive of lack of intention or effort. Non-doing, by contrast, is about where and how intention and effort is focused. There are situations in which paying more attention to this moment is a more powerful strategy than trying to get busy while moving nowhere fast. For example, you may find your mind racing as you feel anxious about your friendship group and thinking about all the possibilities available to you (from leaving university to going home for a weekend or whatever else). The more you think about it the more confused you feel. Emotional anxiety is creating physical effects, perhaps sickness or headaches. In such a scenario there are many tools throughout this book you can use, from looking at your values, managing any Gremlins, working from a place of confidence, being creative about possibilities and looking at relationships in different ways. In addition, though, it might also be that there is a need to let go of the racing mind, over-thinking and sense of urgency, and engage with what is now, i.e. your thoughts, emotions and physical experiences.

Rather like a dancer who is moving with flair through complete awareness of their body, paying attention to 'what is' can ironically lead to powerful transformation and movement. This idea resonates with the question we posed in Part 1, asking yourself 'How am I?' each day. Now though the intention is not to ask such a question with a view to then know how to proceed – it is rather about learning to become aware of what is right now. By learning to pay attention to 'this moment', new possibilities may unfold that previous 'automatic' responses and previous 'noise' may have blinded you to. Instead of paying attention to your thoughts of what could or should be – desiring the past, the future or somewhere else – a reaction to struggling for change can be to ask: What is now? What is right here? What is on offer in this present moment? What is the lecturer saying? What if I look at my friend afresh? How am I experiencing the weather? Food?

Perhaps you've experienced dancing to your favourite music without a thought, writing fluently as the words just find themselves without effort, or played a sport where it's felt so easy you didn't need to try. In these moments you are present. Becoming aware of the present moment, and accepting what is, will enhance the impact of the different activities we suggest throughout the book. It will also save a lot of time and energy that is otherwise taken up in denying and resisting what is present.

How to notice afresh

Being in the moment is something you can learn by cultivating your awareness of your experience in everyday situations. The key is learning to become aware of the physical experience, the thought responses and emotional reactions to a situation in this moment. By practicing being in the moment with different everyday experiences you can develop the ability to enjoy what is now. It is also a powerful way to 'break' habitual reactions to situations.

Take a piece of food that you are familiar with, for example a piece of fruit, or a sweet. Hold the piece of food in your fingers and look at it as if you've never seen it before. Pay attention to how it feels. Allow yourself time to notice its colour, texture, its smell, even its sound. As you do so, notice any familiar thoughts or feelings that arise as you are paying attention. The key word is notice. Don't engage with the thought, or follow it. Notice it as if it was a drop of water coming over a waterfall.

Now, with awareness of your body, bring the piece of food to your lips, allowing it to touch your lips before it enters your mouth. As you do so, notice with as much attention as you can the detailed physical responses as you salivate, the muscles as you chew, the impulse to swallow. Again, notice your thoughts, your emotions as you eat the piece of food. Repeat this several times, each time experiencing the piece of food afresh. Be aware of what you notice.

Tip: a piece of food is a start. You can adapt the above to any situation in your daily life: taking a shower, brushing your teeth, shopping, reading a book, listening to music, walking, cycling. Watching your activities over a period of time is a good way of spotting your automatic responses to situations.

Note: accepting what is now does not mean resigning yourself to a situation. If I don't accept I have broken arm, I may not give it the attention and care it needs to fix it. I'm not resigned to a broken arm. I'm accepting it in order to enable it to heal. So acceptance means being able to engage in the moment and it is from this moment that change will occur. Change is inevitable and by being in the moment, and accepting what is now, you are, ironically, engaging in change.

8.2 Pausing to come back to the moment

One of the problems of enjoying the journey can be how to respond to difficult or challenging situations. Throughout the book there are various tools we've introduced that are helpful both in responding to difficult situations, as well as in avoiding the build-up of difficult situations in the first place. However, there are times when difficult situations emerge and your response to them can mean the difference between life feeling OK at university and a desperate need to leave. When you are in the midst of experiencing a crisis, this is often the time when it is the hardest of all to see the wood for the trees. While sometimes a crisis can bring you very much into the present, it can also be a time when it can be particularly hard to be present, because your mind is racing. It can be hard to experience what is real and to have the wisdom to accept 'what is' in order to move on. You might find yourself losing a sense of awareness and choice and default to responding in ways that may not always be helpful.

Your breath is available to you right now

If you've tried out some of the experiments in this book, you've probably noticed things that you previously responded to automatically, and realised when it's useful to be doing things automatically, and when it's not. When you go to a class with a certain lecturer perhaps you've noticed you get automatic thoughts (e.g. 'Not him again'), feelings (e.g. bored, anticipation) and physical responses (e.g. tired, energised). Similarly, when a friend starts telling you their problems with other friends you find yourself with certain thoughts (e.g. 'He's a stuck record player'), feelings (e.g. anxious) and physical responses (e.g. jittery stomach).

We've suggested various ways throughout the book in which you might 'interrupt' the automatic responses that you don't find helpful (see, for example, Section 4.2 on confidence). In situations where you feel overwhelmed, however, it can be hard to notice them.

One way to make it easier to address automatic responses is to pause, to be able to see more clearly. One thing to know – assuming you are living – is that in whatever situation you find yourself in, you always have access to your breath! That's good news because, and building on the previous section, this means your breath is always available to you as a focus for experiencing the present moment. Not only can focusing on the breath be a relaxing and de-stressing experience in and of itself, it can also

create the space to experience what is in this moment, to observe your
own automated responses in your thoughts, feelings and body, and so
also become able to see choice in how to be and what to do or not to do,
including do nothing.

How to pause and come back to this moment

Breathing spaces provide a short and powerful way to take a break, interrupt
your automatic thoughts, emotions and physical experience and create a clearer
perspective. Key to the process is to cultivate non-judgemental observation
of thoughts, feelings and physical sensations. As a short 3-minute exercise in
mindfulness, the breathing space provides a tool that can be used regularly to bring
yourself to the present moment, as well as a tool to use in response to particularly
difficult or crisis situations.

Sitting down with a straight back and upright posture helps in creating a sense of
focus, though you can also do this lying down or standing up. The key is cultivating
a sense of dignity in your posture as best you can. You'll need a timer that will bleep
every minute for 3 minutes.

In the first minute, become aware of your body, your thoughts and your feelings.
Notice any physical sensations, including where you are touching the ground, any
aches or pains. There is no need to fix them, just notice them. Notice any emotions
you are experiencing. Again, not trying to fix or change them, just observing them.
Accepting them without judgement. Next, notice your thoughts. Your thoughts are not
you, they are thoughts that come and go, like birds flying past. Just observe them and
let them go.

When the first timer sounds, bring your awareness to your breath. The key here is
noticing, not changing. Your breath knows what to do! Allow yourself to notice the air
entering your body and moving into your lungs. Notice how your belly moves in and
out with each breath. And watch as the air leaves your body again. Your mind may
wander. That's OK. When you realise you've wandered, just bring your awareness
back to the breath (and congratulate yourself for noticing!).

In the third minute, become aware of your breath in relation to your whole body.
Imagine the breath giving oxygen to every cell in your body. Where you feel aches or
pains, imagine breathing into them, letting the area expand. At the end of the third
minute, bring your attention back to the room and, as best you can, allow yourself to
keep a sense of your awareness with you through the day.

Tip: this short mindfulness exercise becomes more powerful the more often your practice it. Practicing it five times a day can have quite an impact. It can also work well if supported by longer and more regular mindfulness practices. There are many practices available online which can be found with searches for 'mindfulness of breathing', 'breathing spaces', and 'body scan meditations'.

8.3 Being with your experience and letting go of the story

You may find that when things are not going as you'd like them to be, you get caught up in trying to make sense of what the problem is and not really being able to solve it. For example, you find yourself feeling a little withdrawn at a party, not feeling like dancing and wondering why everyone else seems to have so much fun. At this moment you start asking 'What's wrong with me?' **Stories are just stories** and in come the Gremlins telling you all the things you ought to be doing ('You ought to be having fun', 'You shouldn't be feeling sorry for yourself'). You may feel a little sad. In these situations sometimes it is helpful to work out what's going on. Again, some of the exercises in this book could help. At the same time, however, it can also be detrimental if you find yourself caught in a spiral of asking 'Why?' and trying too hard to find solutions. An alternative strategy is to let go of any story. To let go of trying to make sense of what you are experiencing or even give it any meaning and instead, just observe it.

Just observing an experience, particularly an unpleasant one may seem counter-intuitive. We tend to want to avoid pain or unpleasant things. If you are experiencing something you don't like surely it's better to avoid it or fix it? Sometimes though, the fixes are so temporary and often involve unsatisfactory forms of escape that the feeling comes back, perhaps even more strongly or in another form at a later time. The harder you try to push it away, the more strongly it bounces back. By sitting with the experience, observing it, becoming curious about the experience, ironically, there can be change. Our bodies, our minds and our emotions are all processes, all subject to change. Acknowledging an experience, allowing your body, thoughts and feelings to express themselves can sometimes be the most powerful thing to do.

How to be with your experience and let go of the story

By getting to know an experience, even an unpleasant one, the energy of that experience often shifts. By using a meditation technique, emphasis is placed on non-judgemental observation of the experience, without an attachment to meaning or an outcome. Instead, the focus is on what the experience feels like, rather than what it is about, why it is there or how to make sense of it. You may find you need to meditate several times over a period of weeks.

The start of this is the same as the previous exercise, however we repeat it here to enable you to see the whole meditation in one go.

Sitting down with a straight back and upright posture helps in creating a sense of focus, though you can also do this lying down or standing up. The key is cultivating a sense of dignity in your posture, as best you can. You'll need a timer that will bleep three times at 5-minute intervals (15 minutes altogether).

In the first 5 minutes, allow yourself to become aware of how you are right now, noticing your body, your thoughts and your feelings. Notice any physical sensations, including where you are touching the ground, any aches or pains. There is no need to fix them, just notice them. Then notice any emotions you are experiencing. Again, not trying to fix or change them, rather just noticing them, being curious about them. Next notice your thoughts. Your thoughts are not you, they are thoughts that come and go, like clouds floating by in the sky. Just let them go.

Now bring your attention to your breath. The key here is noticing, not changing. Your breath knows what to do! Allow yourself to notice the air entering your body and moving through into your lungs. Notice how your belly moves in and out with each breath. And watch as the air leaves your body again. Note: your mind may wander. That's OK. Just bring your attention back to the breath and congratulate yourself for noticing! Stay with the breath, and keeping your posture until your hear the 5 minute timer.

In the second 5 minutes, bring awareness to what you have been feeling. Start to notice the physical sensation that the feeling creates in your body. Is it everywhere? Is it in a particular spot? Bring your attention to that sensation. Unless you are superhuman, your mind may wander, following thoughts or other distractions. That's fine. When you notice that happen, simply bring your attention back to the physical sensation. Become curious about the experience, noticing it as if you've never known it before. There is no need to do anything, just to notice it and to keep noticing it until you hear the next 5-minute timer.

In the final 5 minutes, being your attention back to your whole body. Notice your feet, your ankles, shin bones, knees, thighs and hips. Follow your back up to your shoulders. Keeping your posture and sense of dignity, notice your shoulders, arms, down to your elbows and wrists. Your hands, each finger. Notice your head, your eyes, jaw, mouth, neck. Finally in noticing your chest and your belly become aware of your breath as it comes in and out of your body. Keep focusing on the breath. When you hear the final timer, gently become aware of the space around you and keep a feeling of acceptance with you.

At the end of the meditation notice how you are right now. You may find you feel relaxed, agitated or a mix of other things. There is no right or wrong. The key thing is you are learning to observe an experience without attachment to it.

Tip: if you are used to meditation or relaxation techniques, you could extend the middle phase to 10 or 15 minutes.

8.4 Embracing fear

Seeing things afresh and the breathing space are ways of becoming more present and enhancing your sensitivity to your own automatic responses to situations. There are times though when the idea of observing without judgement may feel very challenging. Why would you want to observe without judgement a Gremlin voice, for example?

Indeed, the strategies we've introduced in this book have often been about deciding what's useful or deciding what not to pursue as a thought, activity or feeling and then change it to something more desirable. Again, though, even where something is clearly not desirable, a process of learning to accept what is can often be the key to enabling transformation to take place. For some of you, when it comes to enjoying the journey of your university experience, there may be fears, and the anxiety they can produce, that are getting in the way.

Fears come in different shapes and forms. Here we're not so much talking about physical fears that may involve severe risks. Some fears are also quite productive, motivating you to do something about a situation. Here our focus is rather on those fears that your mind conjures up and leave you feeling a sense of continued underlying anxiety in your university experience and which inhibit your enjoyment. While spotting the Gremlins that create such fears can be a powerful starting point, sometimes you may experience a fear for which it's hard to name and for which there is no obvious thought that is generating it. It might even be that as you've engaged with the different activities on offer through this book you've changed the way you approach things in positive ways and overcome certain fears. 'Feel the fear and do it anyway' as Susan Jeffers book is called, is one way to manage fears very powerfully.

Yet sometimes a feeling of fear can stick and your university experience is dulled by an underlying churn of anxiety that is hard to place. Throughout our coaching experience with students we've noticed that sometimes it's really useful to engage with that fear in a different way. Instead of trying to make sense of it, trying to shift it or even trying to push it away, accepting it and embracing its energy can have surprising results, allowing you to overcome what can sometimes feel a disabling experience.

Note, if you are experiencing severe anxiety or depression you need to seek medical support rather than rely on the exercises here or elsewhere in the book. Your university will have confidential health and well-being services available to you.

How to embrace your fear

The more we try and push a fear away, the stronger it often becomes. Rather like a yapping puppy that wants attention, giving the fear some attention can enable it to become quieter. This visualisation involves accepting the fear and 'welcoming' it as if it were a friend.

In this visualisation you are going to imagine your fear and 'welcome' it in, learning to love it like a friend.

Spend a few moments to take some deep breaths with your eyes closed. Count five on the in breath, and five on the out breath. Take at least five breaths to create a feeling of relaxation.

Picture yourself standing at the top of five steps. At the bottom of the steps you can see a door. What colour is the door? Notice how you are feeling right now. You are about to go down the steps. Notice any resistance you might feel. Pause if you need to for a moment. Then, acknowledging your experience, go to the bottom of the steps, knowing you can turn around and go back up them if you need to.

Now, standing by the door, notice what the door is made of. Notice the texture of the door. There is a handle on the door. What sort of handle is it? What is it made of? Place your hand on the handle. Again, notice any resistance and allow that to be. Pause if you need to.

When you are ready, open the door and notice on the other side a figure. This figure is your fear. Greet it with a smile and say 'Welcome'. Welcome the fear in as if you were welcoming your best friend in for a cup of tea. There is no need to do anything right now. Just notice it. Be curious about what it looks like, sounds like. Be curious as to what you feel.

Now, let the figure become smaller, small enough for you to able to pick it up. Let it also change colour, to a colour of your choice. Let it become another figure, perhaps an animal or object. Something you can hold. Pick it up. Embrace it. Hold it like a new born puppy. Decide where and how you'd like to carry it: you are going to look after it now. You know it has its fears and you will protect it.

In your own time, go back up the stairs. Become aware of your breath. Breath out and in to the count of five. Do this five times. Then bring your attention back to where you are.

Finally, what object could you find that would represent this fear? A stone, a cuddly toy, something else? Carry that object with you for at least two weeks. Get to know it. Become familiar with it. Become aware of your thoughts and feelings around it.

Student experience – Jane

It can be hard learning to live with a feeling that you don't like, and yet sometimes a visualisation can help. Jane had struggled with accepting her depression:

"The request that you learn to love depression seems rather daft at first, not to mention un-doable, however the hope that it would make living a little easier was more than enough of an incentive to give it a try. The idea behind it being that you cannot fear that which you love. For me, I spent a lot of the time when I wasn't depressed waiting for another episode to strike, scared at the prospect of how bad it could get. In short, depression was terrorising my whole life, even when I was well.

Will asked me to imagine walking down a set of stairs, cut into the ground, with a cavern at the bottom behind a door. Behind the door was my depression. When I was ready, I was asked to open the door and to see the shadows inside before condensing them down into something I could love. For me this was a puppy, before bringing him back out into the sunshine.

After the session I had to find a small child's toy that resembled my imaginary puppy, that could fit in my pocket, to carry it everywhere with me and to generally treat it like a puppy. I was still a little sceptical at this point that this would help me to love my depression, but I kept at it, making sure I had my puppy with me everywhere. This even meant getting to uni only to turn round and head back home because I had forgotten him. You can't leave a puppy all day on his own.

It's been about two months now and I still take my puppy with me. My friends think of him as my revision buddy. In truth, he has helped me to see my depression in a different way, love is still too strong a word for it, but I'm not waiting for it to happen any more either.

It's not about making it go away, it's about getting you to stop waiting for it to happen and get on with living. When I've had a depressive episode since this visualisation, I've had someone to go through it with me, to glare at and to hug. It's no fun for him either but it helps me to focus on the fact that it will eventually pass and in the meantime I still have to get on with stuff day-to-day. If you have a dog, then sometimes you're going to have to walk him in the rain and the cold, its generally unpleasant but for the rest of the time, when he behaves and the sun is shining then there is no point waiting for the rain, just enjoy the walk."

8.5   Cultivating gratitude

This feels like a nice place to end this book – with a note on cultivating gratitude. Whether things are going well or not going as you'd like them to be, there is always some value in noticing the things you are grateful for. Sometimes it can feel hard to be grateful. Especially when you feel sad, let down, frustrated, angry or hurt. The good news is, like any other mode of being, you can learn to become more grateful. With practice it becomes easy!

How to cultivate gratitude

The principle here is that you can train yourself to feel grateful in a way that can be uplifting and open you up to the different possibilities of what life has to offer.

Pick an area of your life you feel frustrated by. Now list all the things you can feel grateful for about that area of your life. See if in 5 minutes you can come up with a list of ten things. You can do this for other areas of your life. Notice what it feels like to identify things you can be grateful for.

For the next week, each day, make a list of the things you feel grateful for. This can be an uplifting and pleasant way to end the day.

Further reading

Adrienne, Carol (1998) *The Purpose of Your Life: Finding Your Place in the World Using Synchronicity, Intuition, and Uncommon Sense*. New York: Eagle Brook.

Bach, Richard, and Russell Munson (1970) *Jonathan Livingston Seagull*. New York: Macmillan.

Bridges, William (1980) *Transitions: Making Sense of Life's Changes*. Reading, MA: Addison-Wesley.

Burkeman, Oliver (2012) *The Antidote: Happiness for People Who Can't Stand Positive Thinking*, Edinburgh, Canongate.

Buzan, Tony (1984) *Make the Most of Your Mind*. New York: Linden.

Buzan, Tony (2002) *How to Mind Map*. London: Thorsons.

Cameron, Julia (1992) *The Artist's Way: A Spiritual Path to Higher Creativity*. Los Angeles, CA: Jeremy P. Tarcher/Perigee.

Carson, Richard David (2003) *Taming Your Gremlin: A Surprisingly Simple Method for Getting Out of Your Own Way*. New York: Quill.

Covey, Stephen R. (1989) *The Seven Habits of Highly Effective People: Restoring the Character Ethic*. New York: Simon and Schuster.

Crum, Thomas, F. (1987) *The Magic of Conflict*. New York: Simon & Schuster.

Csikszentmihyayli, M. (1996) *Creativity: Flow and the Psychology of Discovery and Invention*. London: Harper Collins.

Csikszentmihyayli, M. (2002) *Flow: The Psychology of Happiness: The Classic Work on How to Achieve Happiness*. New edition, London: Rider

HH Dalai Lama and Howard C. Cutler (1998) *The Art of Happiness: A Handbook for Living*. London: Hodder and Stoughton.

Dills, Robert, B. (1991) *Tools for Dreamers: Strategies for Creativity and the Structure of Innovation*. Cupertino, CA: Meta Publications.

Frankl, Viktor E. (1963) *Man's Search for Meaning: An Introduction to Logotherapy*. New York: Simon & Schuster.

Gallwey, W. Timothy (1974) *The Inner Game of Tennis*. New York: Random House.

Gallwey, W. Timothy., Edward S. Hanzelik and John Horton. (2009) *The Inner Game of Stress: Outsmart Life's Challenges and Fulfill Your Potential*. New York: Random House.

Gladwell, Malcolm (2005) *Blink: The Power of Thinking without Thinking*. New York: Little, Brown.

Goleman, Daniel (1995) *Emotional Intelligence*. New York: Bantam.

Greene, Melanie (2008). *Mastering Your Inner Critic*. Chichester: Summersdale.

Hackman, J. Richard (2011) *Collaborative Intelligence: Using Teams to Solve Hard Problems*. San Francisco: Berrett-Koehler.

Hodgkinson, Tom (2007) *The Freedom Manifesto*. London: Penguin.

Jeffers, Susan J. (1987) *Feel the Fear and Do It Anyway*. San Diego, CA: Harcourt Brace Jovanovich.

Jeffers, Susan J. (1996) *End the Struggle and Dance with Life: How to Build Yourself up When the World Gets You down*. New York: St Martin's.

Kabat-Zinn, Jon (1991) *Full Catastrophe Living, How to Cope with Stress, Pain and Illness Using Mindfulness Meditation*. London: Piatkus.

Kabat-Zinn, Jon (2004) *Wherever You Go, There You Are*. London: Piatkus.

Kahneman, Daniel (2011) *Thinking, Fast and Slow*. New York: Farrar, Straus and Giroux

Kimsey-House, Henry, Karen Kinsey-House, Phil Sandahl and Laura Whitworth (2011) *Co-active Coaching: Changing Business, Transforming Lives* (3rd edition). Boston MA: Nicholas Brealey Publishing.

Kumar, Satish (2002) *You Are Therefore I Am: A Declaration of Dependence*. Totnes: Green Books.

McDermott, Ian and Len O'Connor (1996) *NLP and Health: Using NLP to Enhance Your Health and Well Being*. London: Thorsons.

McDermott, Ian and Wendy Jago (2002) *The NLP Coach: A Comprehensive Guide to Personal Well-being and Professional Success*. London: Piatkus.

Nhat Hanh, Thich (2004) *Peace Begins Here: Palestinians and Israelis Listening to Each Other*. Berkeley, CA: Parralax Press.

Peck, M. Scott (1993) *The Road Less Travelled*. London: Rider.

Peters, S. (2012) *The Chimp Paradox: The Mind Management Programme for Confidence, Success and Happiness*. Vermillion: London.

Prior, Robin, and Joseph O'Connor (2000) *NLP and Relationships: Simple Strategies to Make Your Relationships Work*. London: Thorsons.

Scott, Susan (2002) *Fierce Conversations: Achieving Success in Work and in Life, One Conversation at a Time*. London: Piatkus.

Seligman, M. (2002) *Authentic Happiness: Using the New Positive Psychology to Realize your Potential for Lasting Fulfillment*. New York: Free Press.

Tolle, E. (2004) *The Power of Now: A Guide to Spiritual Enlightenment*. London: Hodder.

Tzu, Lao (1963) *Tao Te Ching*. London: Penguin.

Whitmore, John (2002) *Coaching for Performance GROWing People, Performance and Purpose*. London: Nicholas Brealey.

Williamson, Marianne (1992) *A Return to Love: Reflections on the Principles of a Course in Miracles*. London: Harper-Collins.